I0220660

SCROLL SAW INLAY BOXES

made easy

volume 1

A hands on approach to creating
uniquely beautiful boxes with the scroll saw

Thomas H. Haapapuro Jr.

Dedication

This book is dedicated yet again to my wife, Erin L Hubbs-Haapapuro, for the support and patience she gives me each and every day. This book is also dedicated to my family, for the assistance they have all made to my development along the way. Thank you.

A special thanks to Ron Oszuscik. Ron has been a customer of my wood working pattern website for several years. Ron sent me images of the projects he created using my patterns. I was so impressed with his craftsmanship and attention to detail that I asked him to contribute finished projects for this book. Many of the boxes shown in this book were created by Ron's skilled hands. Thanks Ron. What a great job! He advised me that he would love to hear from other wood workers anytime to discuss wood working and the beautiful wood crafts he creates. His e-mail address is rho@nconnect.net.

Finally, I want to thank Jet Tools. They kindly supplied us with their incredible 22" scroll saw for this book. I have never used a more amazing, versatile, and powerful saw. A full review of their saw is included later in this book. Thank you for your support.

This book, the patterns, photographs, and all information presented within this book is the sole intellectual property of Thomas H. Haapapuro Jr, first published in 2017 by Thomas H. Haapapuro, Jr. Readers may make copies of the patterns for personal use. The patterns are not to be duplicated for resale or distribution under any circumstances. Any such copying or duplication is a violation of copyright law.

Product & Process photography provided by Thomas H. Haapapuro Jr.
All rights reserved.

Working with wood, and the tools used to work it, is inherently dangerous, especially if the tools are used incorrectly. Some images were shot in a manner best suited for clarity of the process, and may not represent the safest way to operate the tools. Neither the author nor the publisher assumes any liability for the safety of the reader. This book is sold without warranties or guarantees of any kind, expressed or implied, and the author disclaims any liability for any injuries, losses, or damages caused in any way by the content of this book or the reader's use of the tools needed to complete the projects presented herein. The author urges all readers to thoroughly review each project and to understand the use of all tools before beginning any project. Safety is the most important skill of any woodworker.

about the author

Thomas Haapapuro is a registered landscape architect and an artist. His art work spans a variety of materials, forms, and uses. He is particularly fond of using native wood from salvaged trees. These materials connect people with the landscape and the flora of the local environment, and reduce the carbon footprint in the process of making art.

Originally from the rural Appalachian foothills of eastern Ohio, this natural environment fused in him a deep appreciation of natural shapes and forms, which inform his work.

This is the third book by Thomas. His first book, *Fresh Designs for Woodworking* by Fox Chapel Publishing, introduced readers to his scroll saw based wood art. His second book, *Sculptural Boxes Made Easy*, introduced readers to creating sculptural boxes using basic wood working tools. He has also written several articles for Scroll Saw Magazine.

Thomas also creates a line of organically shaped carved wood bowls which are in private collections throughout the United States. To see these bowls, visit www.modernwoodbowls.com

Thomas runs a website where additional wood working patterns are available for sale. www.modernwoodpatterns.com,

Thomas lives with his wife Erin in Charlotte, North Carolina.

Introduction

No time spent in the wood shop is wasted. This is a private place. A place filled with unlimited potential for exploration, contemplation, and creativity. I love stepping into my shop. The first thing to greet you is the smells, a mix of the sweet scents of lumber and sawdust and the subtle undertones of machine oil from well used and cared for tools. This is not a place of instant gratification. It is a place where a human strives, using their hard earned experiences, skills, and creativity to create a new thing. A special thing. They create in that space a thing that is a stamp of themselves, of what they value and what they can contribute. A monument of what they are and have achieved. A symbol for time forward that they existed.

I love the art of wood working. And I love to envision new projects and share them with the world so that others can be inspired to create useful and beautiful things. Objects that are often gifts to loved ones. Objects that will last. Objects treasured and handed down through generations.

I love to spread the joy and excitement of making a new thing.

I hope you, gentle reader, find pleasure in the process of making the boxes shown in this book and that the recipients of the boxes you create find a pleasure in your craftsmanship.

TABLE OF CONTENTS

3   **Introduction**

6   **Before We Begin**

10   **Step by step box**

22   **The rest of the boxes**

Project Guide

Butterfly Box (Step by Step)
page 10

Bee Box
page 22

Mitosis Box
page 24

Reaching and Grasping Box
page 26

Infinite Radiance Box
page 28

Sublime Radiance Box
page 30

Convergence Box
page 32

Florality Box
page 34

Floral Array Box
page 36

Radial Mitosis Box
page 38

Parallel Universe Box
page 40

Vitality Contained Box
page 42

Vitality Unleashed Box
page 44

Interplay Box
page 46

Vitality Unleashed Box
page 48

BEFORE WE BEGIN

Before getting started, it is helpful to go over the basics of the tools and materials we will be using throughout the book.

Tools

We will be using several different types of tools to create the boxes in this book, but most of them are tools that are typically present in most wood shops. The primary tool we will be using is the scroll saw. The scroll saw is one of the most useful and versatile tools available to the wood worker. We will also use, in limited ways, the band saw, a belt table sander, and a drill or drill press. With these tools, every box in this book can be created.

Below is an overview of the tools and how they will be used:

Scroll Saw

The scroll saw is one of the most unassuming but powerful wood working tools available to wood workers. Often seen as a tool for cutting smaller projects like fretwork, intarsia and other detailed wood work, the scroll saw has a some definite advantages:

- **Finger safe**: The worst injury likely with this little saw is a minor finger cut, and that only if you are being particularly reckless.

- **Thin kerf:** The blades on a scroll saw are much thinner than a band saw blade. Hence, the kerf (the gap left by the saw blade in the cut wood) is much narrower. This is advantageous for inlay work. The thinner the kerf, the less putty filler will be needed and the better looking the inlays.

- **Tight corners:** Even with an 1/8" blade on the band saw, it can only turn 1/8" radius, which is fine for some projects, but it is still a limitation. With the scroll saw and the right blades, there is virtually no restriction on the size turns that can be made. This feature is what makes the intricate outside edges of the boxes in this book possible.

- **Inside cuts**: This is the primary advantage of the scroll saw over any other tool. With a scroll saw, a hole can be drilled into the wood and the blade threaded through it. This will allow the cavity in the box to be cut and will be used to make the inlays.

Band Saw

The band saw is a staple of the wood shop. For this book, it will mostly be used to mill lumber to the needed thickness. It will also play a crucial step in creating the lid catch that will align the lid with the body of the box.

Regarding blades, since the band saw will be used solely to rip cut lumber (and the lid catch), a wider blade is best, typically 1/2" to 3/4". The wider blade aids in getting a straighter rip cut, leaving less warp in the cut and a cleaner project. Select a blade that has the highest TPI (tooth per inch) available. More teeth means a somewhat slower cutting rate, but it gives a much cleaner, smoother cut.

Planers

Re-sawn wood, rip cut wood, and oversized wood will all need to be milled flat with a planer. Most of the projects will require boards that are 1/4" in thickness. I typically rip cut a board to about 3/8" then plane down to 1/4" to ensure that the board is smooth and flat on both sides without any tooth marks from the rip cut.

Sanding

Ughh. Sanding. To many wood workers, sanding can be the most tedious part of the wood working experience. However, I have met a few who actually enjoy the Zen like process of sanding. To those of you who find sanding a satisfying and calming activity, good for you. Let me know if you want to sand some of my work.

For the rest of you, sanding can be made a lot less time consuming by using a power sanding system. There is not a lot of sanding needed for scroll saw boxes. Typically, its a little clean up on the edges of the box if things got a little wonky or if there is a burn mark from a too hot blade. In these cases, I like to use a power sander.

There are many of these on the market, but the sanders from King Arthur Tools are my favorite.

Their Guinevere sander is a sanding system built around a motor and a flexible shaft. The system uses pneumatic sanding drums with sanding sleeves. The drums come in many different sizes and shapes, allowing the wood worker to power sand nearly any corner, nook or cranny. Power sanding saves a lot of time and energy, and allows the wood worker to move quickly past this daunting step in the wood art process.

Due disclosure. After using the KA Tools products for years in my wood work and articles, they invited me to represent them at a local wood working tool expo. Since I already loved their product line, I agreed. Many years on, I continue to represent their tools at wood working shows. I now know the people who operate this family business, and we have a great relationship. But no matter how wonderful the people and the company is, it all started because I fell in love with the amazing high quality tools they make. I recommend their tools not because of my relationship with the company, but because the tools really are the best suited to the projects.

Belt Sander Table

For a few key steps, a belt sander makes life a lot easier. Even easier if that belt sander is a table model. We will use this tool to flatten the inlays after they are installed, to remove the remnants of the paper patterns, and to remove the rip cut marks from the lid catch. This tool isn't necessary. It just makes things easier.

Accessories

In addition to the tools and the wood, there are several other items that will be helpful in creating the boxes. A brief list is provided below:

Glue

All the boxes will need to be glued. Every wood worker has their preference, and mine is Titebond II. It has a fast initial tack, a relatively quick curing time, and it is strong.

Double Sided Tape

A quality paper based double sided tape is absolutely critical to creating these boxes. In this book, it is typically used to temporarily hold pieces together as they are cut and then separated again. This technique is used in every project in this book. Double sided tape can be purchased at any wood working store, though I have always purchased mine from Klingspor Wood Working Shop (www.woodworkingshop.com)

KLINGSPOR'S
WOODWORKING SHOP
"Quality Tools and Supplies for the Woodworker"

Sharpened Putty Knife

Related to the double sided tape is the sharpened putty knife I use this to separate the pieces of wood held together with the double sided tape. I find that a metal putty knife, sharpened to a knife edge on a whetstone, is perfect to separate pieces of wood that are taped together. The thin edge nicely gets between the layers of wood, and the narrow blade allows the pieces to be pried apart without damaging or denting the wood.

Clamps

A wood worker can never have enough clamps. For this book, clamps will be used routinely as pieces are glued together. My preference is bar clamps as they screw down to create a very tight bond between wood pieces.

Tool Review
JET TOOLS 22" SCROLL SAW

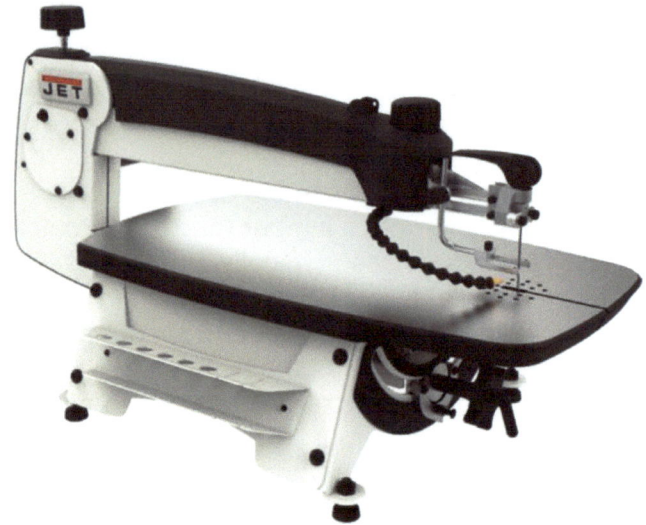

Have you ever driven a luxury car after driving an economy car for a while? Both cars will get you where you need to go. But the luxury car makes the trip far more enjoyable. That is the difference between the Jet Scroll Saw and other saws I have used. You can (I have) use lesser saws to make wood art. Any working scroll saw can be used to make boxes, but a nice saw, like the Jet, makes the process a lot more enjoyable. The saw has many high end features, including a large throat clearance, minimal vibration, a powerful motor, easy blade changes, and positive stops at typical table angles. None of these are strictly necessary to create beautiful scroll saw boxes. But they sure make the process a lot easier and a lot more fun. Below is a brief summary of the highlights of this saw that I found while using this saw to write this book.

Throat Clearance

22" throat depth. Wow. I cannot count the number of times on my previous saw that I had to back out of a cut when the work piece unexpectedly caught up on the back of the saw. With 22" of throat depth, the Jet saw made this issue a thing of the past for all but my biggest projects. It is not necessary to have this much clearance, but it sure is a nice feature.

Vibration (or the lack thereof)

The table on the Jet Scroll Saw is cast iron. A cast iron table is the difference between a workable saw and an amazing saw. The extra weight and density absorbs the vibration, allowing for smooth, straight cuts without the work piece bouncing all over the place.

Another nice thing about this saw is they removed the insert around the blade. Many saws have a disposable plastic insert that mounts in the table. Jet removed this, and just made the table the support around the work piece. I was not sure about this change at first. But the opening is small enough that even fine details and small pieces receive the support they need. This is a nice innovation.

Blade Changes

This is the most unique aspect of this saw and what drew me to this saw when i first saw it. Installing new blades is both tool-less and doesn't happen under the saw. The blades are mounted in a cylindrical blade holder that you can hold in your

hand. How does this work? Let me explain. The bottom of the blade is secured in the detachable blade holder. To install a new blade, unscrew the knob a few turns and insert the bottom of the blade. Turn the knob to finger tighten the blade into place. One end of the blade holder is machined to fit into a little wrench built into the saw stand. Insert that end of the blade holder into the wrench to secure it, then twist to

tighten the blade into place.
Once the blade is secured, the blade holder then slips right into a spring loaded receiver under the saw table. From there, swing the blade up and into the top lock, turn the knob there to lock that end of the blade in place, and you are done.

This truly is the coolest part of the saw. No more looking for the blade change tool and no more squinting under the table to make sure the blade is getting installed correctly. The whole operation can happen in your hand, then slip it into place once the blade is loaded. I don't mean to over state this, but the blade changes are super cool.

The saw comes with several spare blade holders, so you can load a variety of blades into different holders. This allows you to switch blade types quickly and easily. For the boxes in this book, I used two blade types. A thicker, more robust blade for cutting the thicker wood pieces of the box bodies, and a smaller, thinner blade for stack cutting the inlays. Having a couple pre-loaded blade holders with different blade types ready to go made the whole process seamless.

Speed control

This is a variable speed saw. Like most saws the speed can be adjusted by a control knob on the saw itself. One additional option that Jet thought of though was including a foot pedal to start and stop the blade, saving you from reaching up to turn the saw off between cuts and blade changes. Pretty fancy right? I have been using the luxury car metaphor for this review. That the saw actually comes with a foot pedal just locks it in.

Summary

Jet has made a quality tool here. It is solid design with all the aspects you expect from a higher end saw - cast iron table, large throat clearance, minimal vibrations. But it is also an innovative saw. The blade changes really are useful. And adding a foot pedal, while not strictly necessary, is a nice feature. My overall opinion? Its a nice saw. If you were thinking of upgrading, this is the one.

THE PROJECTS

All of the boxes in this book follow the same basic process. To begin, this book will walk the reader step by step for one particular box, providing detailed images and instructions for each part of the build. The rest of the book will be more concise, leaving out the steps that are standard, but will show the steps that are different and unique to each box to guide the reader along.

WOOD USED:
Box Body - Walnut & Maple
Inlay- Maple
Box Top and Bottom - Walnut

7 1/16"

5 5/16"

BOX TOP

INLAYS (TYP.)

PERIMETER OF BOX

EDGE OF WOOD BLOCK

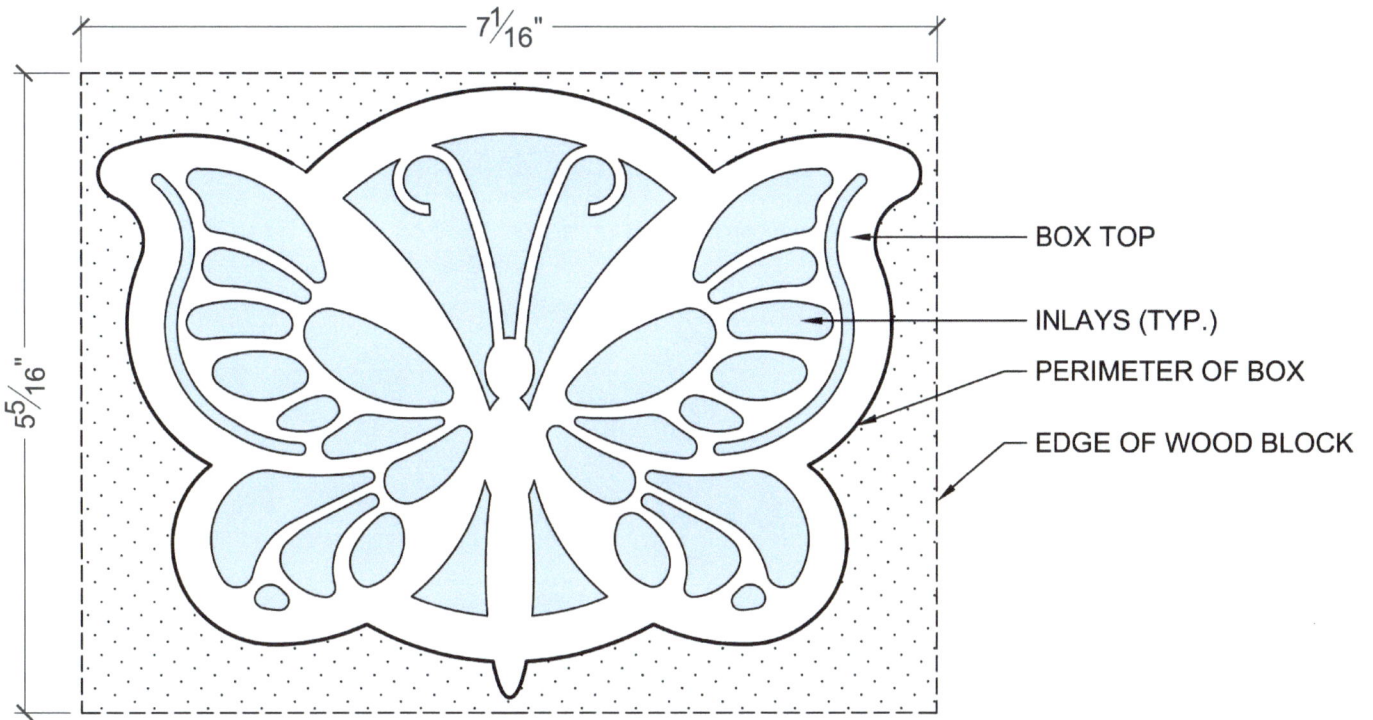

BUTTERFLY BOX
PATTERN A (INLAY)

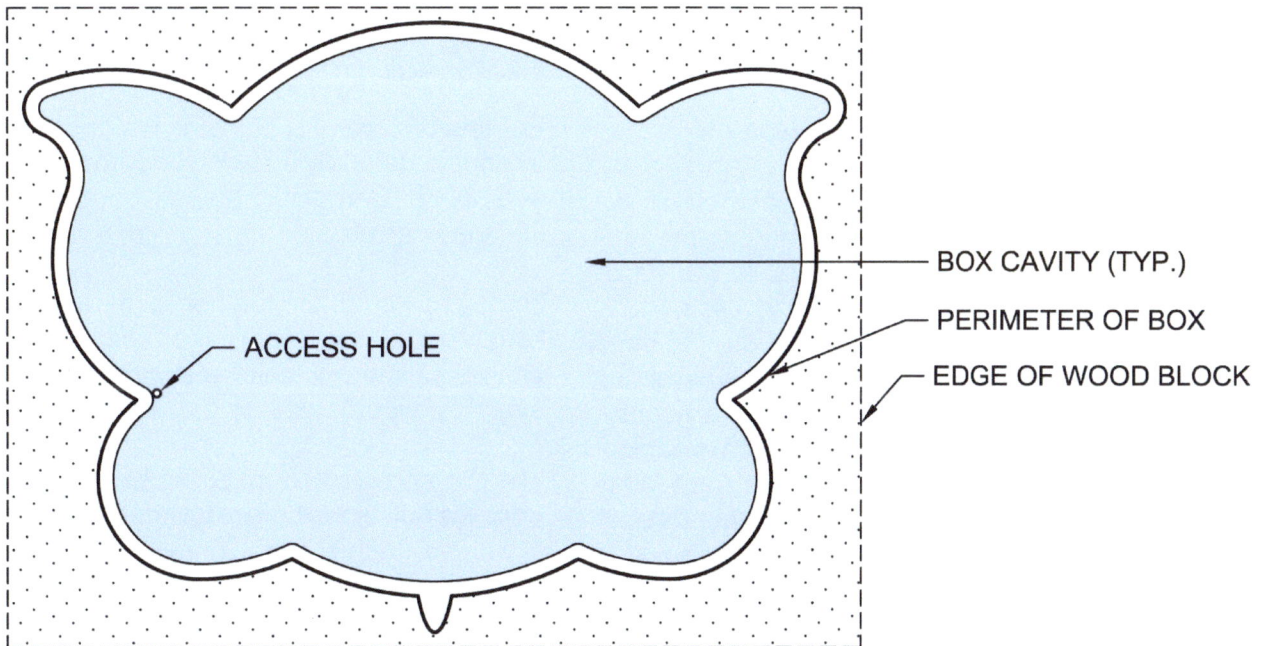

BOX CAVITY (TYP.)

PERIMETER OF BOX

EDGE OF WOOD BLOCK

ACCESS HOLE

BUTTERFLY BOX
PATTERN B (BOX CAVITY)

Building the box

This process of building this box applies to every box in this book. The steps are exactly the same for every other box. To simplify things at first, we will use just two types of wood. In later boxes, we explore using a variety of woods for different inlays to accentuate the patterns.

material you could make the box blank 2" thick (1/4" bottom + 1/4" top + 1-1/2" body = 2" thick box blank). However, it is still a good idea to leave a little room between the box blank and the top of the blade, so I recommend a 1-3/4" box blank for a 2" capable saw. If your saw cuts less than 2", adjust the box body material to accommodate your particular saw.

1. PREPARE THE LUMBER

To prepare the lumber for the body of the box, the first step is to determine the maximum depth of cut your particular scroll saw allows. To maximize the cut on most saws, it is usually necessary to remove the hold down clamp on the saw. To check the maximum depth of cut, push the saw arm down. Then, using a ruler, measure the amount of blade from the blade clamp down to the table. This is the maximum cut depth of your saw. Most saws are about 2" to 2-1/2". This determines how deep your box can be. This needs to be kept in mind when preparing the lumber for the box.

The box will be a composed of a bottom board, the box body, and the lid of the box. Together, we will call this the box blank. The top and bottom boards will be 1/4" thick each (minimum, this reduces warping). If your saw can cut 2" thick

For this box, we will be using walnut and maple. Walnut is naturally a dark wood and maple is near white. Combining these woods makes a very striking contrast.

To begin, we cut the lumber to the approximate length and width given in the pattern, The sizes can be adjusted to suite your preference and available wood supply.

The top and the bottom of the box will be made from walnut. These pieces should be milled to about 1/4" in thickness. To mill the lumber, cut it to the size shown in the pattern. Using a band saw, re-saw the lumber to about 3/8". Run the wood through a planer, planing both sides until the wood is about 1/4" in thickness.

At the same time, cut the inlay board. This will be the same length and width as the walnut boards.

It will also need to be the same thickness as the lid of the box so that the inlays are level with the lid.

For the body of the box, we will assume the depth will be 1-1/4" thick. This piece could be made by gluing together two 5/8" boards. This approach is used in several boxes in this book. For this particular box, we will be making the box body with a contrasting stripe in the middle. This can add a very attractive element to the side of the box. In this scenario, we will plane 2 pieces of maple to a thickness of 1/2" and a single piece of walnut to 1/4".

2 ASSEMBLE THE BOX BLANK

Once all the lumber is cut to size and milled to dimension. the box body can be glued together. For this box, this is the two maple pieces and the center walnut stripe. Add glue in a concentric ring to ensure even coverage and a tight, uniform bond between the pieces.

Clamp the pieces tightly together, and let dry for an hour.

The top and the bottom of the box blank will be attached using double sided tape. Put the tape on the top of the box body, then attach the top 1/4" board. Flip the blank over and repeat the same step to attach the bottom. To ensure a secure bond, clamp the entire blank together and set aside for a few minutes. Then remove the clamps.

Finally, time to do some sawing. Use a blade that works well with cutting thick material. This is a matter of preference, but a thicker blade with fewer teeth generally works best. Also, choose a skip tooth blade. The missing teeth allow saw dust to be pulled out of the cut as the blade moves up and down. This lets the cut breath and will lead to less scorching. Some people also find placing plastic packing tape on the bottom of the box blank reduces scorching.

From the outside of the box blank, cut toward the edge of the pattern. Take your time making this cut. Thick wood can be slow to cut on a scroll saw. The important thing to remember is do not rush the cut. Let the blade cut. Forcing the cut faster than the blade is cutting can result in a bowed cut and scorching of the side of the box. If your saw is a variable speed saw, set the speed at medium. Running it too fast can also result in scorching.

3. ATTACH THE PATTERN

The next step is to attach the pattern, noted as "Pattern A" for this box and all boxes in this book. Make a copy of the pattern on a copy machine. Cut the pattern out. Using a light duty (sometimes called re-positional) spray adhesive, spray the back of the pattern (do not spray the adhesive on the wood. the wood is very absorbent which will make it harder to remove the pattern later. It can also affect the finish later on.) Wave the pattern in the air for a few seconds so the adhesive begins to tack, then adhere the pattern to the top of the box blank.

When you get to a corner, let the saw run in place for a few seconds. Even if you are being very patient, the top of the blade is probably still a little ahead of the blade at the bottom of the cut. If you turn too fast at a corner, the top of the cut will look fine, but the bottom will be bowed or rounded. So let the blade idle in place for about 5 seconds so that the bottom of the blade can catch up with the top of the blade. Then, rotate the work piece and continue the cut.

4. CUT THE OUTSIDE OF THE BOX

5. SEPARATING THE PIECES

Before we begin cutting the cavity into the box, the top and bottom of the box need to be separated from the box blank.

First, use a pencil to mark the side of the box. I typically draw a "V" that extends from the top of the box down to the bottom. This will help keep track of the up and down sides of the pieces and also helps align the pieces during later assembly.

Using a metal putty knife, gently separate the walnut top piece from the box blank. Be careful not to dent or damage the wood when inserting the putty knife. Repeat this step to remove the bottom walnut piece from the box blank.

6. ATTACH PATTERN B.

Make a copy of Pattern B. This pattern will be used to guide the cut for the box cavity. As before apply spray adhesive to the back of the pattern. The pattern has the exact outside pattern that pattern A had. This will help to align the pattern. Hold the box body up to a strong light source. This will make the paper translucent and will help align the pattern.

An alternate method would be to use a pair of scissors to carefully cut the outside of the pattern. This method would also work to align the edge of the pattern with the outside edge of the box body. I personally think this takes a bit too much time, but it is a viable alternate.

Once the pattern is aligned, rub the pattern a few times to create a tight bond between the pattern and the wood.

7. DRILL THE ACCESS HOLE

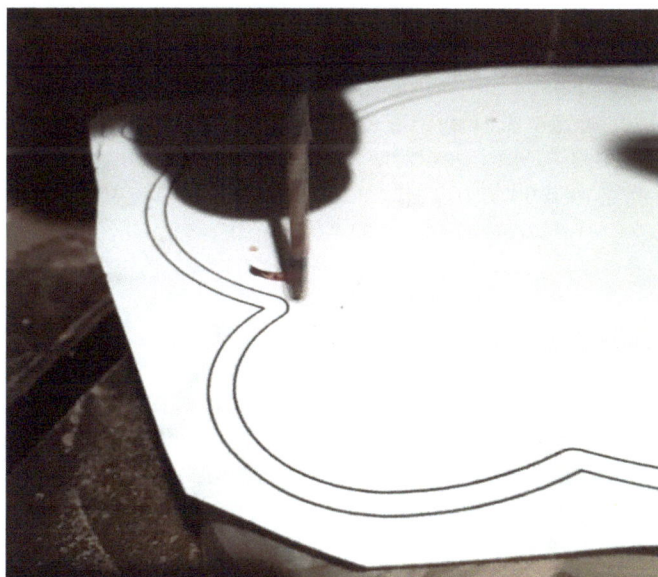

An access hole will need to be drilled into the center of the box body. The pattern shows an ideal location for this hole. Use a drill press so that the hole is perpendicular to the box body.

8. CUTTING THE BOX CAVITY.

This is what makes a scroll saw such an amazing tool: the blade can be threaded into a work piece. Use a blade for thick material. Thread the blade into the pilot hole and lock the blade in place.

Cutting the cavity is exactly the same as cutting the perimeter of the box, except that this cut is a little easier as the work piece has been reduced by 1/2" since the top and bottom boards have been removed. This will make it go a little faster. But it is even more critical now that the cut does not exceed the capacity of the blade. If the blade bulges during this step, it could cause the cavity material to become locked in place, making it impossible to remove the cavity material, and ruining the box. Take your time. As before, pause at corners where the blade changes direction to allow the bottom of the blade to catch up to the top of the blade.

When the box cavity cut is complete and you have returned to the access hole, turn off the saw and gently remove the blade from the cut. The box cavity waste material should easily slide out from the main box body.

9. CUT THE LID CATCH

The lid catch for the box will be made from the top of the box cavity waste material. This is best done using a band saw. Set the fence on the band saw about 1/4" from the blade. Turn the cavity waste material on its edge with the face (the part that still has the pattern paper on it) up against the fence. Hold the piece very firmly, pushing the piece down toward the table. Very carefully and very slowly, feed the work piece into the band saw blade. **WARNING.** This step can be dangerous. The work piece has various edges and rocking points. If the work piece is not held firmly and pushed hard toward the table, it is possible for the work piece to twist into the blade unexpectedly, with worrisome results. Be very careful, mindful, and wary during this step.

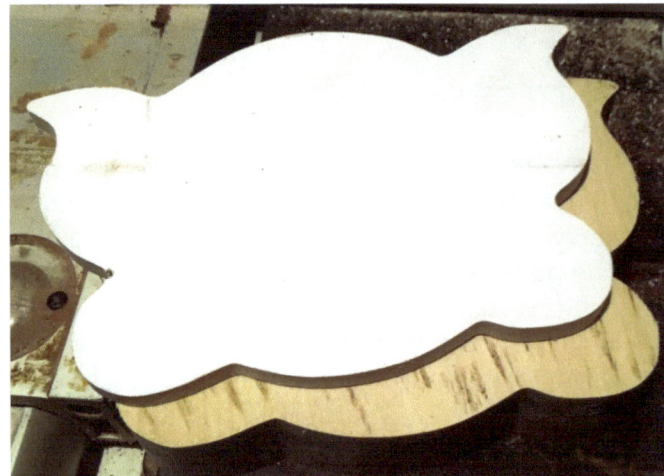

When the cut is complete, remove the paper pattern from the top of the lid catch. The other piece of wood is waste material, and can be discarded.

10. CUTTING THE INLAY.

Finally, the inlay step. This step will use the top of the box (it should still have pattern A attached to it) and the inlay piece of maple that was milled earlier.

Apply double sided tape to the back of the top piece of the box. Attach this piece to the inlay piece. Make sure the grain runs in the same direction. Clamp the piece together for a few minutes to ensure a tight bond between the two pieces.

Holes will be needed to feed the scroll saw blade into the work piece. Select the smallest drill bit you have. Drill a hole at the inside edge of the inlay pieces. Drill through the walnut board and clear through the inlay board beneath.

Insert in the scroll saw a blade suited for finer details. A small, thin blade is best for this step. The thinner the kerf the better. Thread the blade into the work piece through the access holes. This step should be relatively easy to cut since the work piece is only 1/2" thick.

The blade should be perpendicular to the table. Some inlay techniques have the table tilted so that a snug and seamless inlay is created. This technique requires that each cut be made in the same rotation (clockwise/counter clockwise.) This technique does not work well with complex shapes like the ones shown in this book. So for all the boxes in this book, assume the blade is perpendicular to the work piece.

At a medium speed, cut the inlays from the work piece. As each inlay stack is cut free, set them aside in a bowl or other safe place.

When all of the inlays are cut free, separate the box top from the inlay board. The inlay board can be discarded.

The maple inlays will still be attached to the walnut pieces above with double sided tape. Separate the pieces. Discard the walnut inlays and remove any remaining double sided tape from the top of the maple inlays.

11. ASSEMBLING THE INLAY LID

Since we cut the inlays at the same time we cut the holes in the lid, any variation that occurred cutting the holes was also reflected in the inlays below. So the inlays will fit perfectly no matter how carefully the pieces were cut.

Set the lid face down on a waste board. Insert the maple inlays, also face down, into the appropriate holes. Just dry fit the inlays into the box lid. Do not use glue. The inlays will be glued in place when the lid catch is added.

When all of the inlays are in place, lower the box body onto the lid (still face down on the table). Use the pencil marks on the side to ensure the body is precisely aligned with the lid underneath.

It is time to attach the lid catch that was cut from the cavity waste material earlier. Make sure the top of the lid catch is facing down. A test run at this time is a good idea. Apply glue to the top side of the lid catch and spread the glue evenly with a putty knife. Avoid getting glue on the sides of the lid catch as that part will be visible.

With the glue side of the lid catch pointing down, drop the lid catch into the box body. It slide easily down to rest against the bottom of the lid. Use your fingers to press the lid catch firmly onto the lid. Let this set for a few minutes to allow the glue to get an initial tack.

Gently lift the box body from the work piece. The box lid should still face down on the waste board. This will hold the inlays in place while the glue is drying. Let the glue sit for a few more minutes to develop an initial tack. Then, lift the waste board and the lid from the work surface enough to slip the clamps into position. Clamp the piece tightly, and set aside to dry. Add a few clamps to ensure that the lid is pressed tightly all the way around. When the lid catch is dry, the inlays will be locked in place.

12. ASSEMBLING THE BOX BODY

While the lid is drying, the box can be assembled. Apply a thin line of glue to the bottom of the box body. (Make sure it is the bottom, check your pencil marks!) Use a finger to smooth the glue into an even sheet.

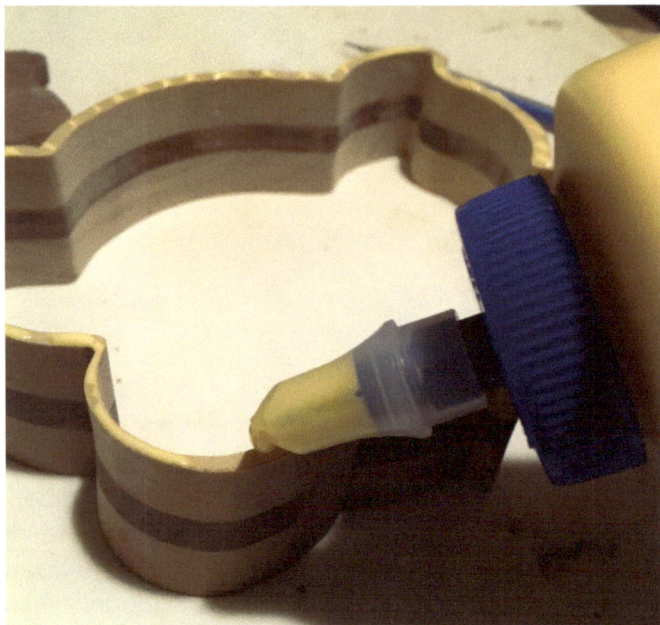

Place the walnut box bottom onto the bottom of the box cavity. Make sure the pencil registration marks line up. Move the pieces around carefully to ensure that the box cavity and the bottom are precisely aligned. When you are sure that they are, clamp them together and set aside to dry.

13. COMPLETING THE LID

When the glue up on the lid has cured, remove the clamps. The pattern is still attached to the top of the lid. We will now use a belt sander table to remove the pattern and ensure that the inlays and the box top are perfectly flat.

Load a course grit belt onto the sander table. Hold the lid by the sides, and gently, evenly lower the lid onto the running belt. The sander can be aggressive, so lightly push the lid onto the belt. Make sure the grain of the wood is running in the direction of the running belt. Sand until the pattern is gone being careful to not over sand. You can also use the belt sander to flatten the bottom of the lid catch if it is rough from the rip cut made with the band saw.

There is a lot of debris around the inlays. Use an air compressor to blow all the sawdust, glue dust, and pattern paper from the sides of the inlays.

The technique used to create inlays in this book is versatile and allows for a variety of shapes to be inlaid. The drawback though is that there is a gap left around the inlays (the kerf) made by the sawing. There is also a hole in each inlay from the pilot holes. This can be remedied with the use of wood putty.

Select a putty color that matches the color of the inlay, in this case, maple. I used Minwax Natural Pine for this box which is close in tone to the color of the maple.

Apply a dab of it to the top surface of the box. Push the putty downward into the kerf. Avoid getting putty on the sides of the box as that will require clean up in the sanding stage.

Use a putty knife to scrape away any extra putty left on the surface. When the box is fully covered, set aside to dry.

When the putty is dry (usually a day later), sand the top of the box to remove any extra putty. You should now be left with a thin line of putty around each inlay that blends into the inlay material. At this point, finalize the box by sanding all the pieces. Sand to at least 220 grit.

14. FINISHING

Finishing is a matter of preference. I typically use either linseed oil or a polyurethane spray. For this box, I decided to go with the polyurethane spray. Spray a light coat. Let dry. Sand with fine steel wool, and spray again.

And the box is complete. These exact steps are all you need to complete all of the boxes in this book.

BEE BOX

WOOD USED:
Box Body - Walnut & Maple
Inlay- Maple
Box Top and Bottom - Walnut

5¼"

5¼"

BOX TOP

INLAYS (TYP.)

PERIMETER OF BOX

EDGE OF WOOD BLOCK

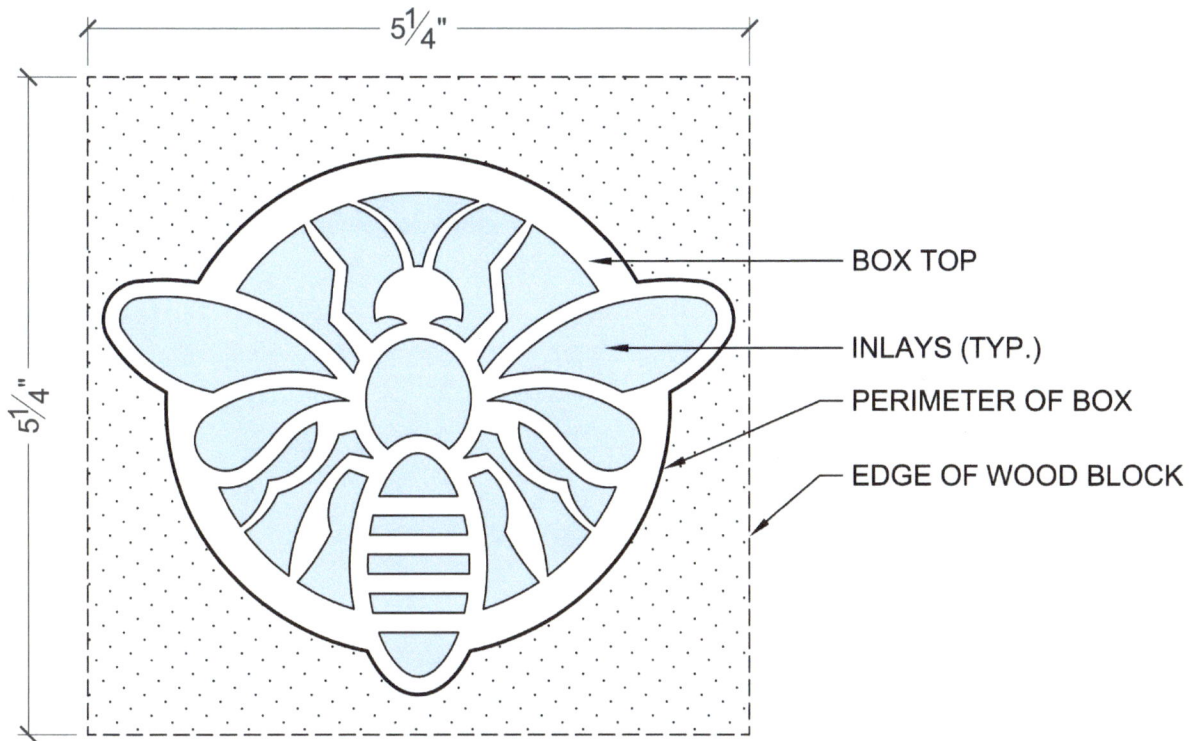

BEE BOX
PATTERN A (INLAY)

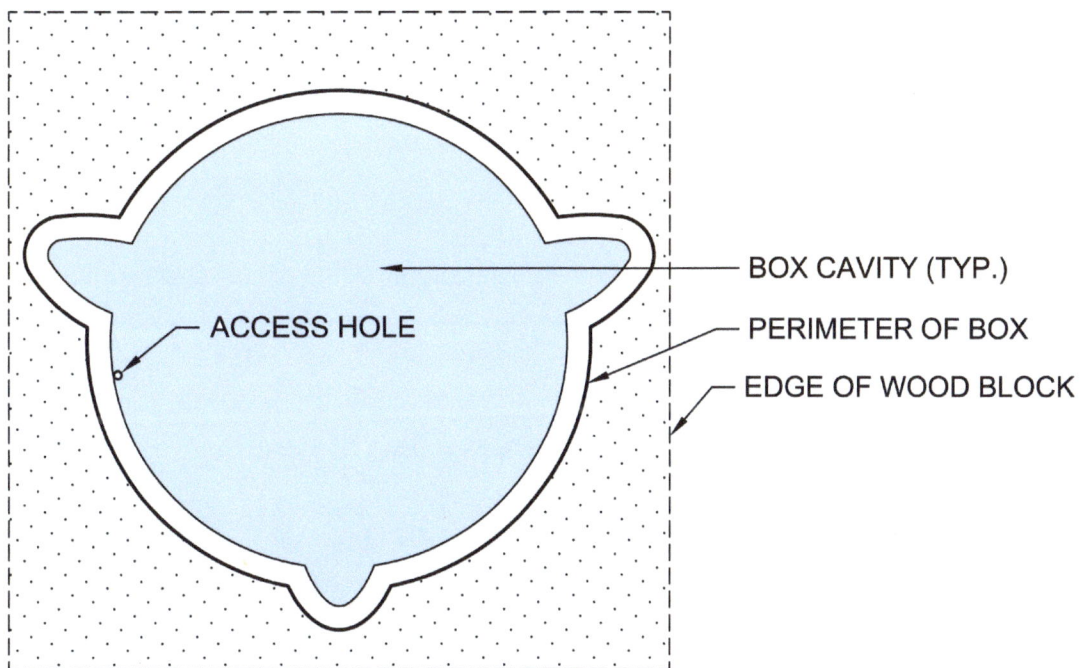

BOX CAVITY (TYP.)

PERIMETER OF BOX

EDGE OF WOOD BLOCK

ACCESS HOLE

BEE BOX
PATTERN B (BOX CAVITY)

MITOSIS BOX

WOOD USED:
Box Body - Maple
Inlay- Blue Pine
Box Top & Bottom - Leopard Wood

6⅛"

8¼"

INLAYS (TYP.)

PERIMETER OF BOX

EDGE OF WOOD BLOCK

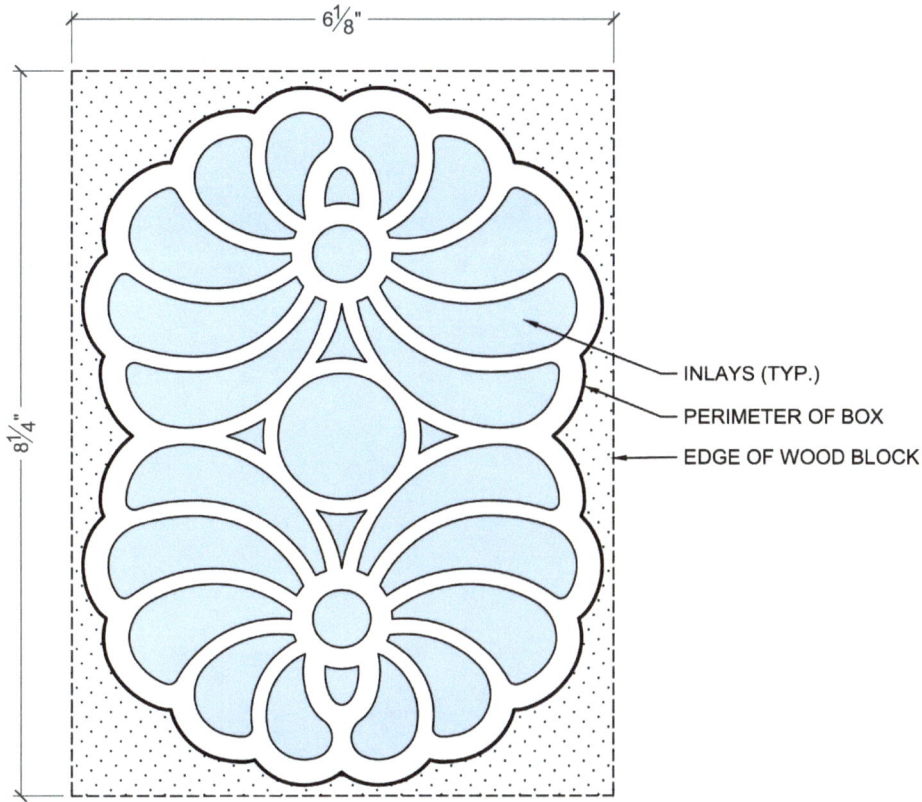

MITOSIS BOX
PATTERN A (INLAY)

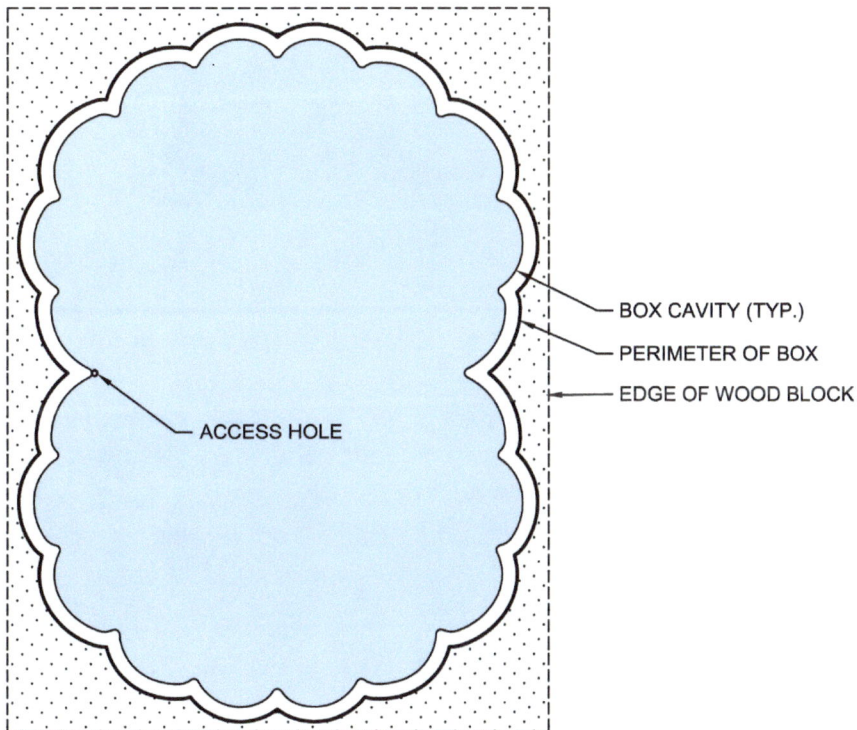

BOX CAVITY (TYP.)

PERIMETER OF BOX

EDGE OF WOOD BLOCK

ACCESS HOLE

MITOSIS BOX
PATTERN B (BOX CAVITY)

REACHING AND GRASPING BOX

WOOD USED:
Box Body - Oak
Inlay - Lignum Vitae
Box Top & Bottom - Red Box Elder

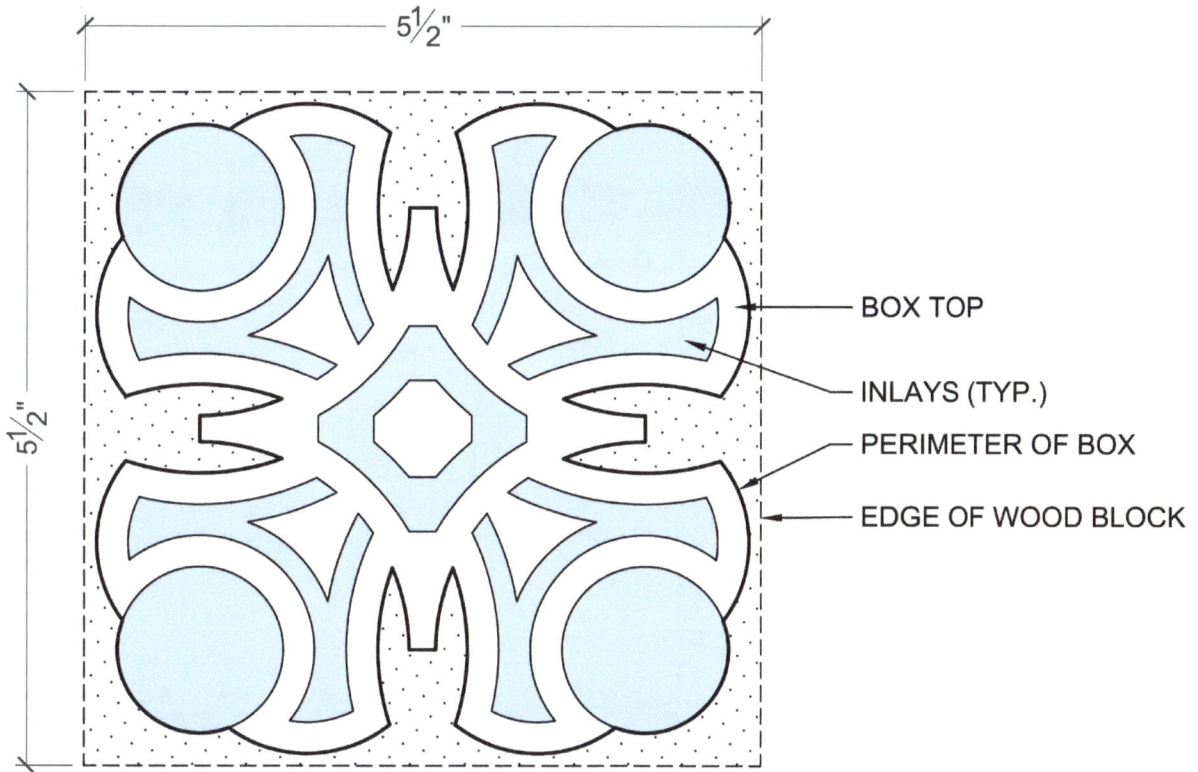

5½"

5½"

BOX TOP

INLAYS (TYP.)

PERIMETER OF BOX

EDGE OF WOOD BLOCK

REACHING & GRASPING BOX

PATTERN A (INLAY)

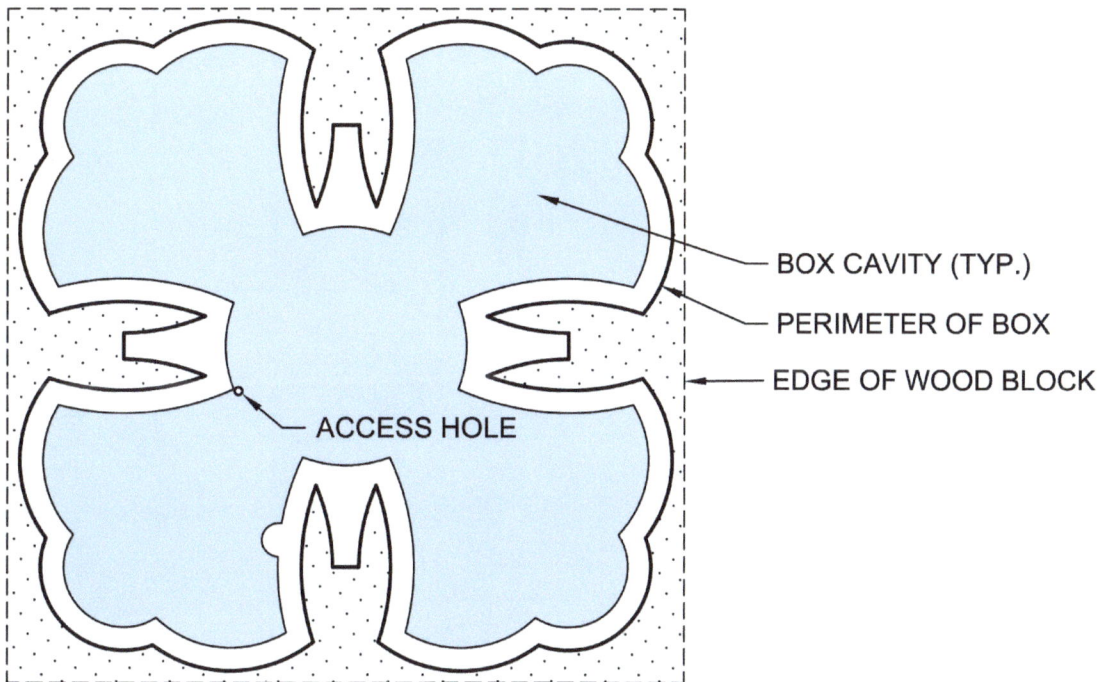

BOX CAVITY (TYP.)

PERIMETER OF BOX

EDGE OF WOOD BLOCK

ACCESS HOLE

REACHING & GRASPING BOX

PATTERN B (BOX CAVITY)

INFINITE RADIANCE

WOOD USED:
Box Body - Oak
Inlay 1 - Blood wood
Inlay 2 - Walnut
Box Top & Bottom - Curly Cherry

6¼"

6¼"

OUTER INLAY (OUTLAY?)
(3 TOTAL)

INLAYS (TYP.)

PERIMETER OF BOX

EDGE OF WOOD BLOCK

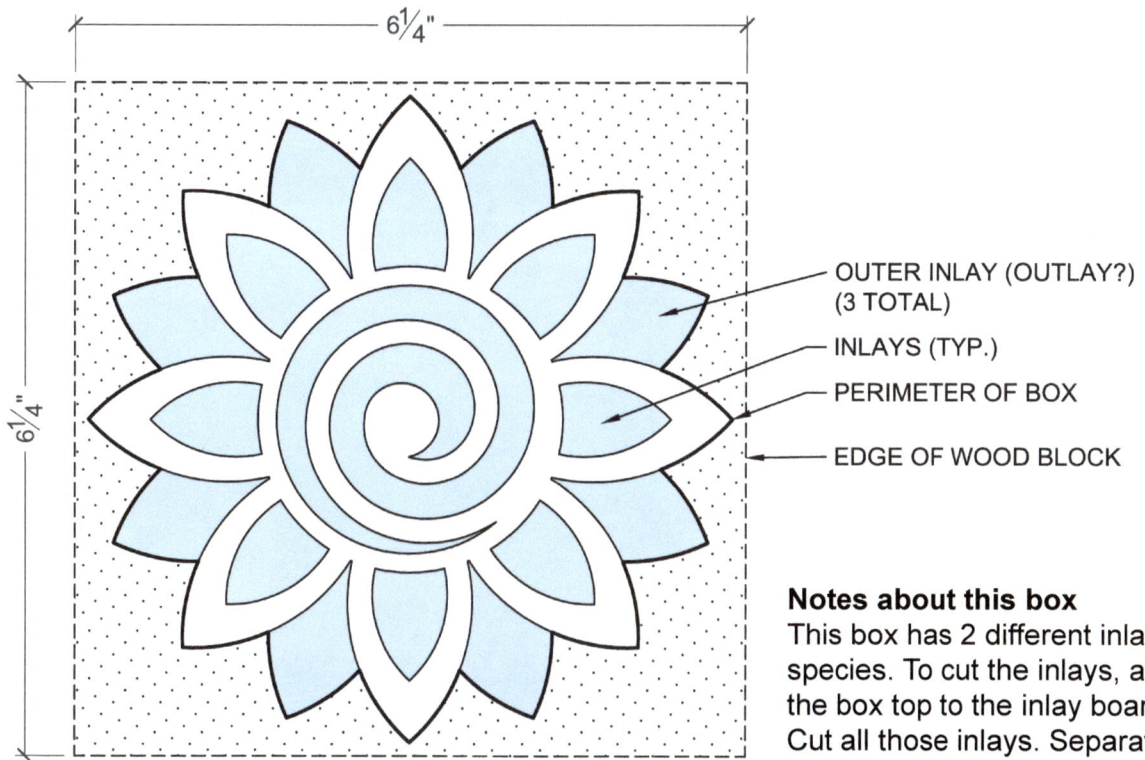

INFINITE RADIANCE BOX
PATTERN A (INLAY)

Notes about this box
This box has 2 different inlay species. To cut the inlays, attach the box top to the inlay board 1. Cut all those inlays. Separate the box top from the inlay board, and then attach inlay board 2. Cut the remaining inlays.

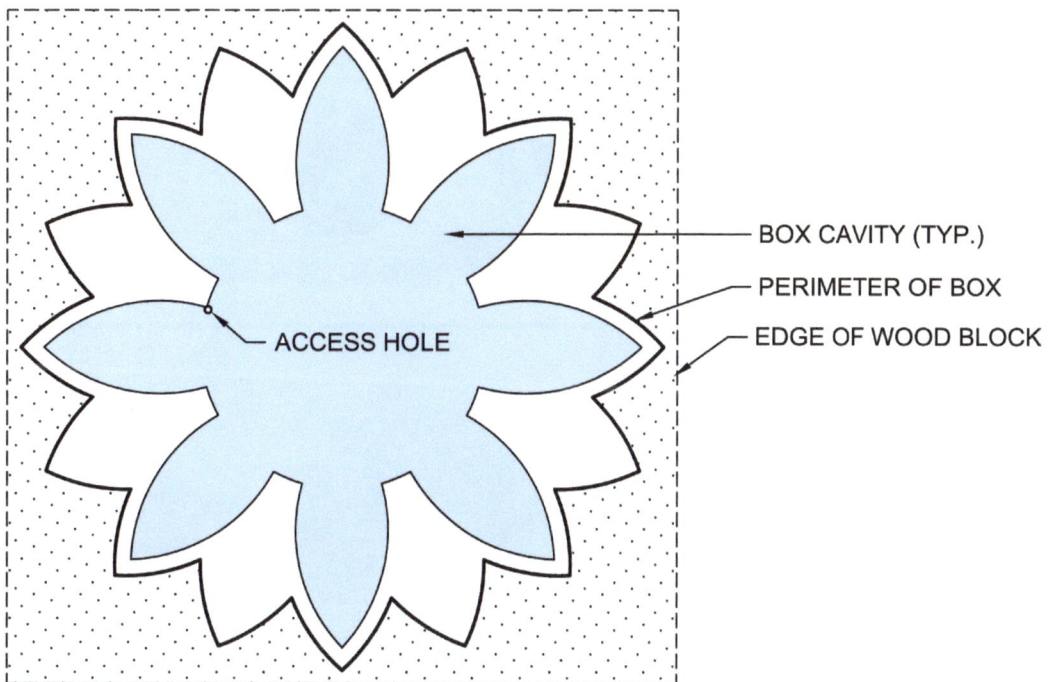

BOX CAVITY (TYP.)

PERIMETER OF BOX

EDGE OF WOOD BLOCK

ACCESS HOLE

INFINITE RADIANCE BOX
PATTERN B (BOX CAVITY)

SUBLIME RADIANCE BOX

WOOD USED:
Box Body - Honey Locust
Inlay 1- La Cote
Center Inlay- Banksia Pod
Box Top & Bottom - Yellow Heart

5½"

5½"

INLAYS (TYP.)

PERIMETER OF BOX

EDGE OF WOOD BLOCK

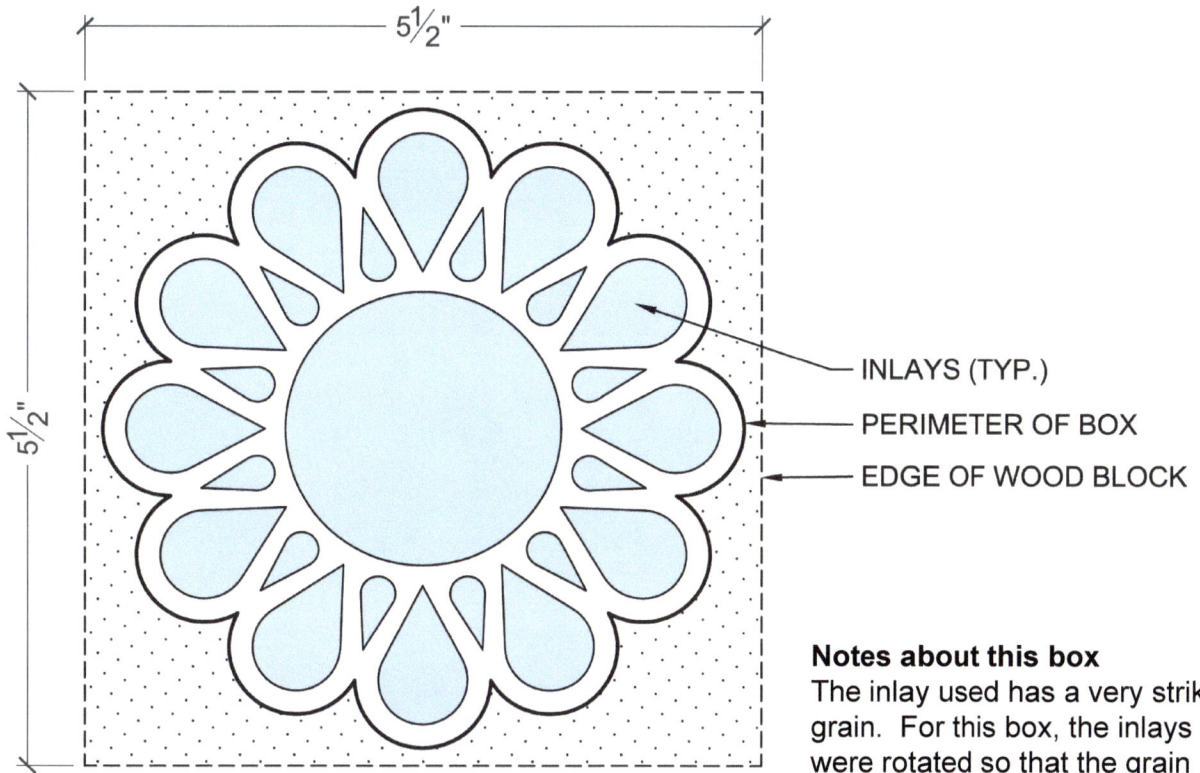

SUBLIME RADIANCE BOX
PATTERN A (INLAY)

Notes about this box
The inlay used has a very striking grain. For this box, the inlays were rotated so that the grain radiates from the center. To do this, separate the inlay board from the box top after every cut, and align with the pattern. Numbering the pieces as they are cut will help during the assembly stage.

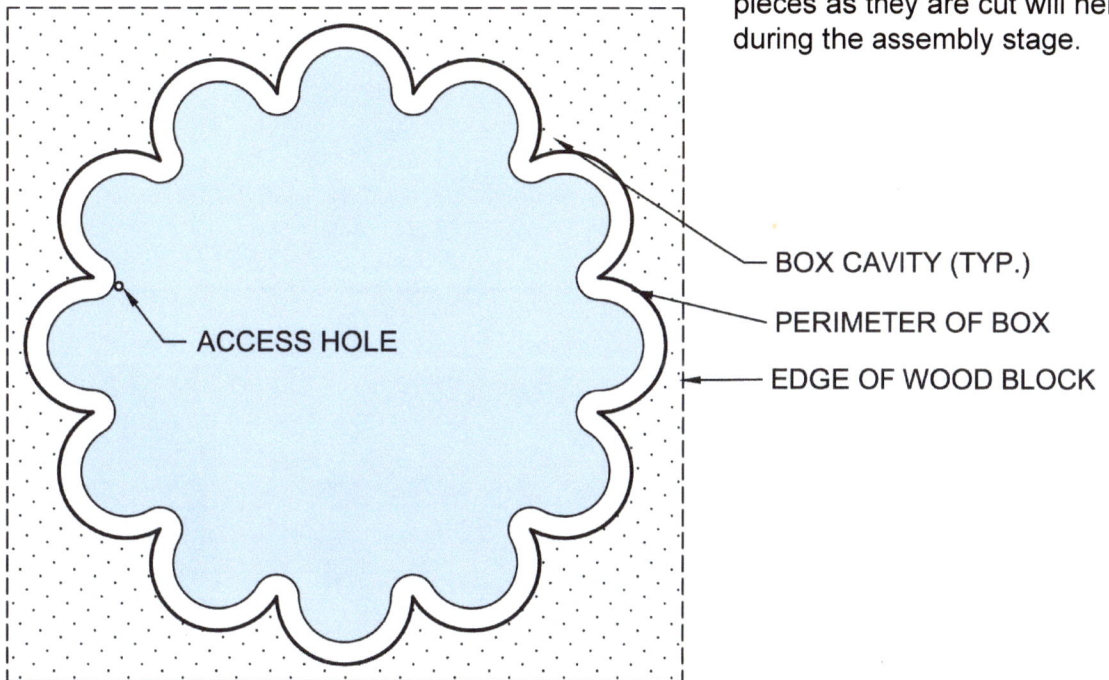

ACCESS HOLE

BOX CAVITY (TYP.)

PERIMETER OF BOX

EDGE OF WOOD BLOCK

SUBLIME RADIANCE BOX
PATTERN B (BOX CAVITY)

CONVERGENCE BOX

WOOD USED:
Box Body - Poplar
Inlay 1- Purple Heart
Inlay 2- Osage Orange
Inlay 3- Lignum Vital
Inlay 4- Holly
Box Top & Bottom - Curly Maple

6¼"

6¼"

BOX TOP

INLAYS (TYP.)

PERIMETER OF BOX

EDGE OF WOOD BLOCK

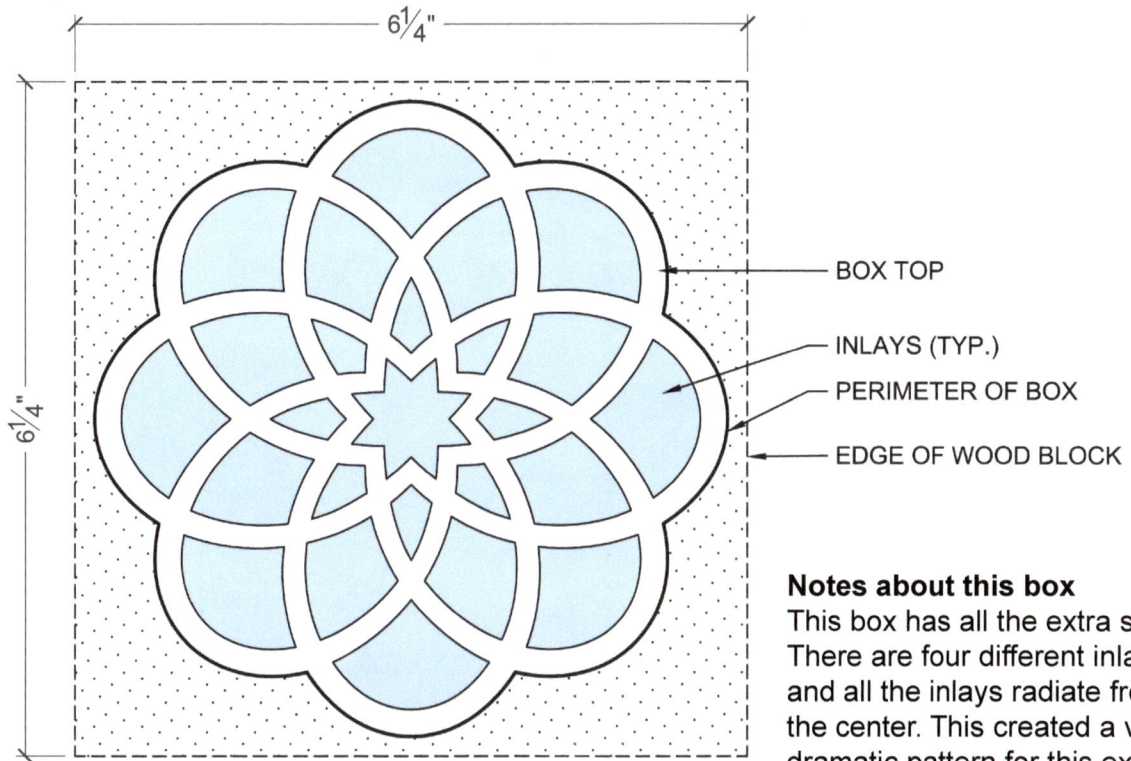

CONVERGENCE BOX
PATTERN A (INLAY)

Notes about this box
This box has all the extra steps. There are four different inlays and all the inlays radiate from the center. This created a very dramatic pattern for this execution of the pattern, though a simpler walnut and maple combination would also look amazing.

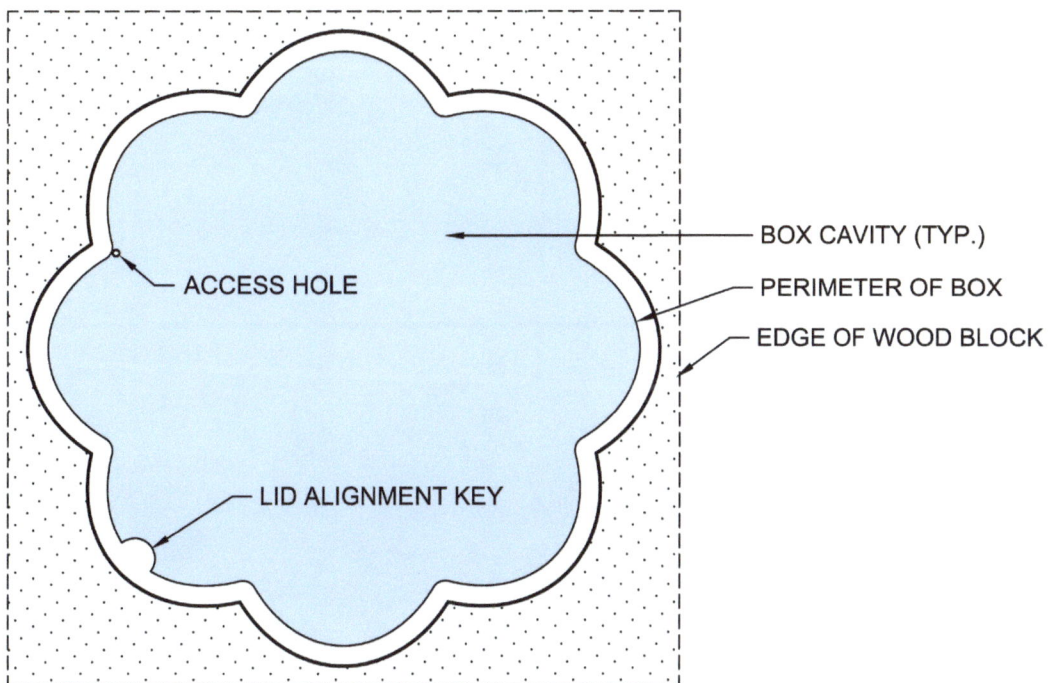

ACCESS HOLE

LID ALIGNMENT KEY

BOX CAVITY (TYP.)

PERIMETER OF BOX

EDGE OF WOOD BLOCK

CONVERGENCE BOX
PATTERN B (BOX CAVITY)

FLORALITY BOX

WOOD USED:
Box Body - Ambrosia Maple
Inlay - Wenge
Box Top & Bottom - Leopard Wood

5½"

5½"

INLAYS (TYP.)

CUT OFF THESE PIECES
(5 TOTAL)

PERIMETER OF BOX

EDGE OF WOOD BLOCK

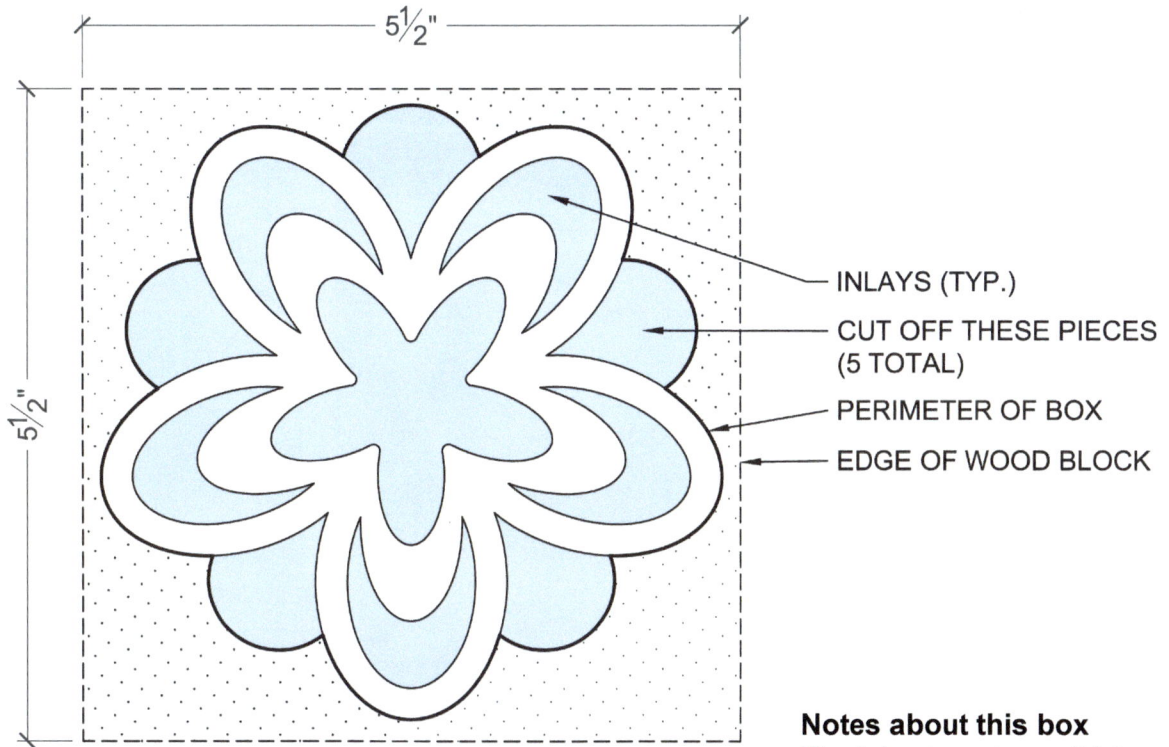

FLORALITY BOX
PATTERN A (INLAY)

Notes about this box
The inlay board was thicker
than the box top. This makes
the inlays pop out of the top
of the box. These were then
rounded with a sanding drum.
This effect can be very striking.

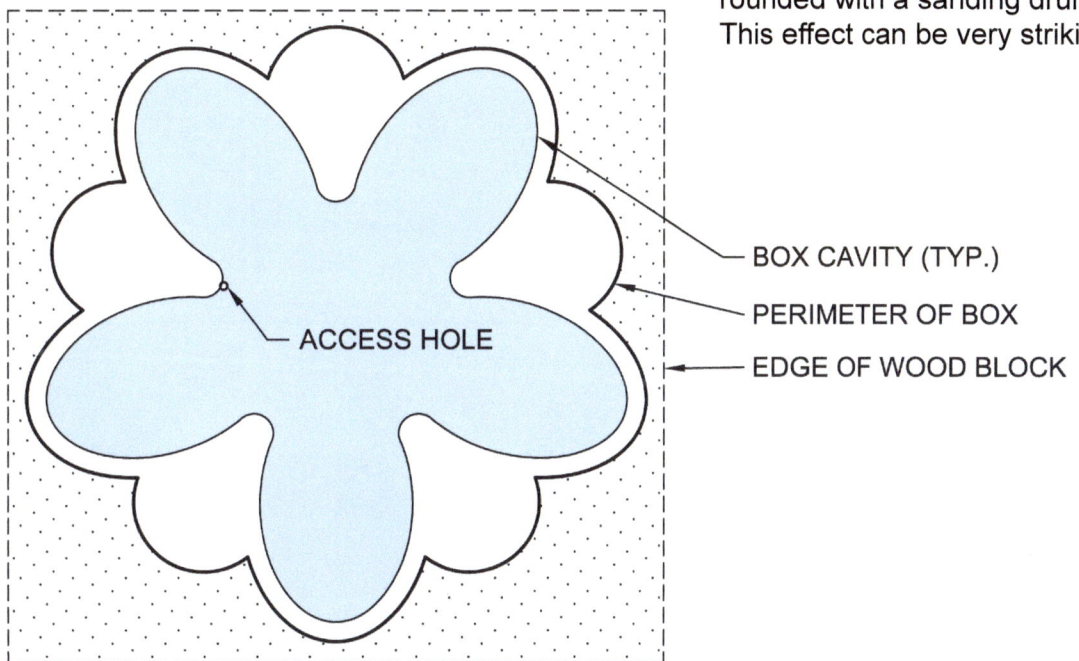

ACCESS HOLE

BOX CAVITY (TYP.)

PERIMETER OF BOX

EDGE OF WOOD BLOCK

FLORALITY BOX
PATTERN B (BOX CAVITY)

FLORAL ARRAY

WOOD USED:
Box Body - Ash
Inlay 1 - Yellow Heart
Inlay 2 - Holly
Inlay 3 - Laminate (various species)
Box Top & Bottom - Mahogany

6"

6"

BOX TOP

INLAYS (TYP.)

PERIMETER OF BOX

EDGE OF WOOD BLOCK

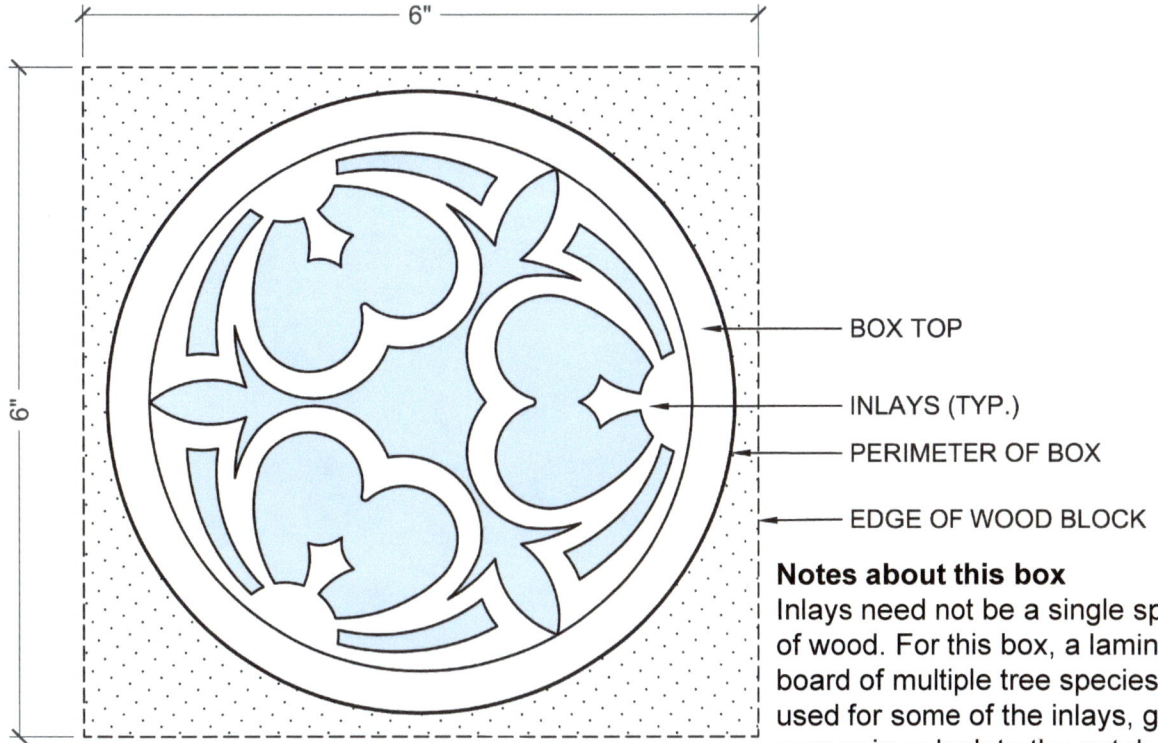

FLORAL ARRAY
PATTERN A (INLAY)

Notes about this box
Inlays need not be a single species of wood. For this box, a laminate board of multiple tree species was used for some of the inlays, giving a very unique look to the petals of this box.

Side note. This pattern was based on three flower petals around a central point. However, my wife saw it as two people kissing I decided to run with that story for her.

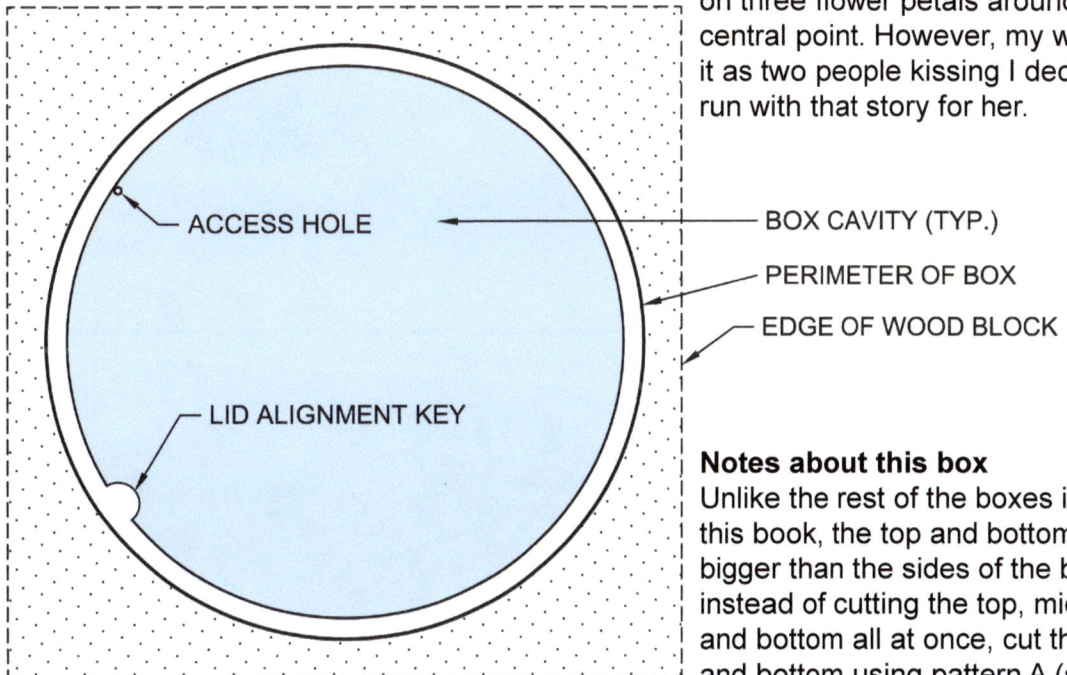

ACCESS HOLE

LID ALIGNMENT KEY

BOX CAVITY (TYP.)

PERIMETER OF BOX

EDGE OF WOOD BLOCK

Notes about this box
Unlike the rest of the boxes in this book, the top and bottom are bigger than the sides of the box. So instead of cutting the top, middle, and bottom all at once, cut the top and bottom using pattern A (stack cut them using double sided tape). Cut the outside and inside of pattern B separately for the box body.

FLORAL ARRAY
PATTERN B (BOX CAVITY)

RADIAL MITOSIS BOX

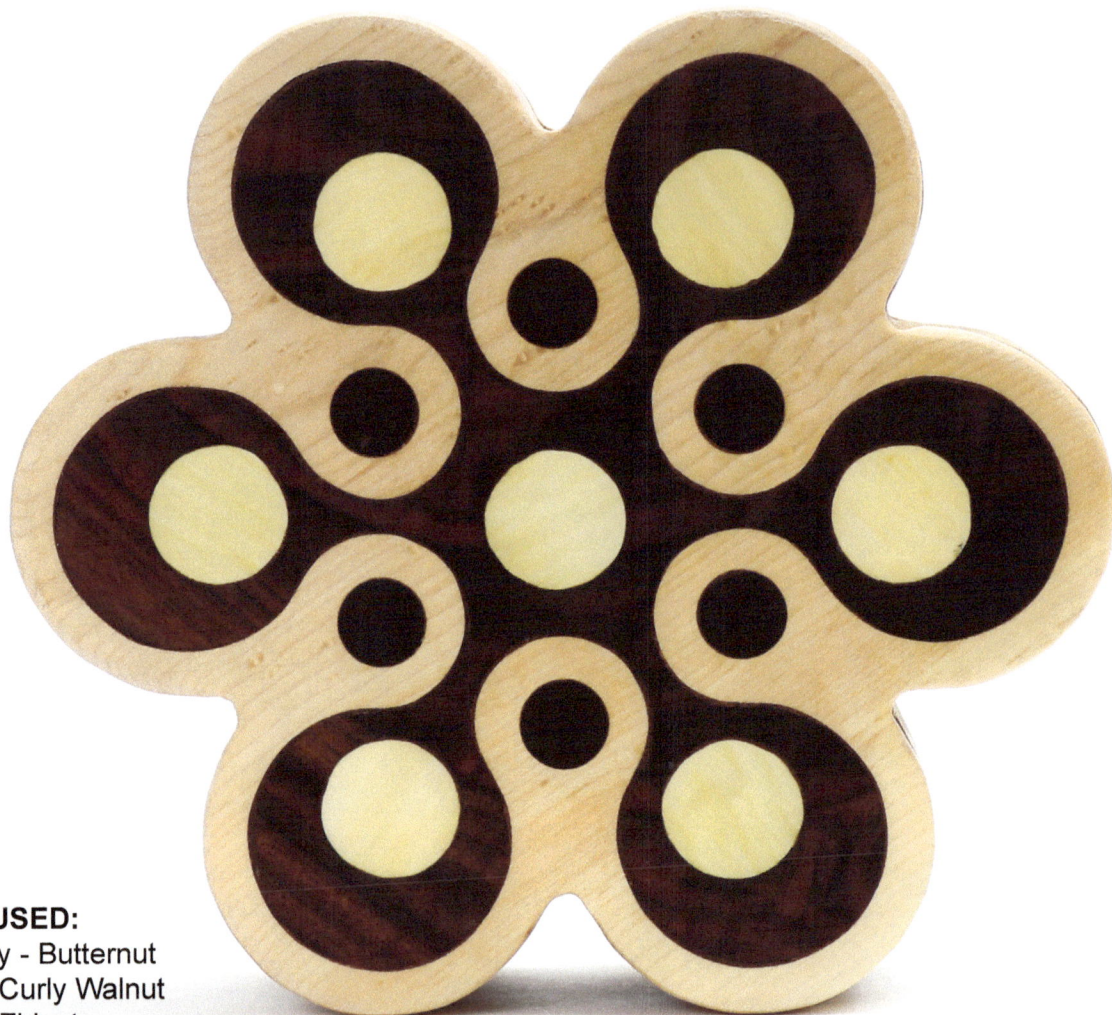

WOOD USED:
Box Body - Butternut
Inlay 1 - Curly Walnut
Inlay 2 - Ziricote
Inlay 3 - Holly
Box Top & Bottom - Bird's Eye Maple

6"

6"

BOX TOP

INLAYS (TYP.)

PERIMETER OF BOX

EDGE OF WOOD BLOCK

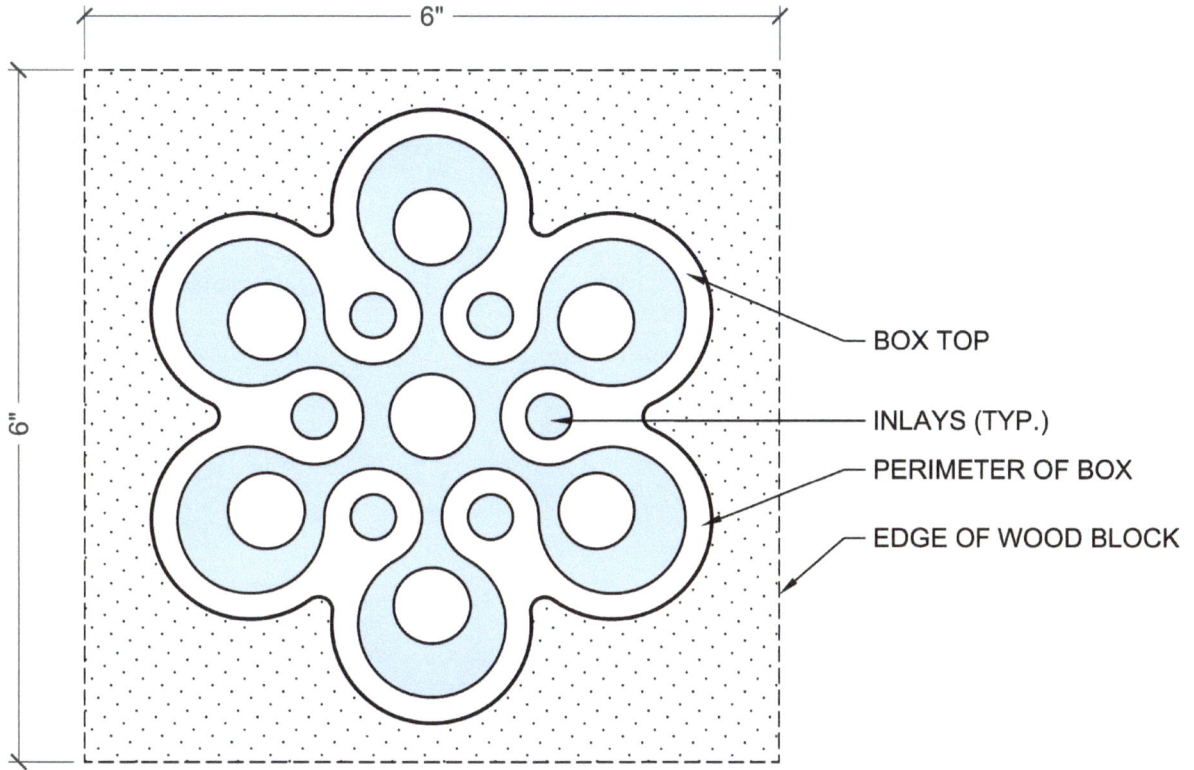

RADIAL MITOSIS
PATTERN A (INLAY)

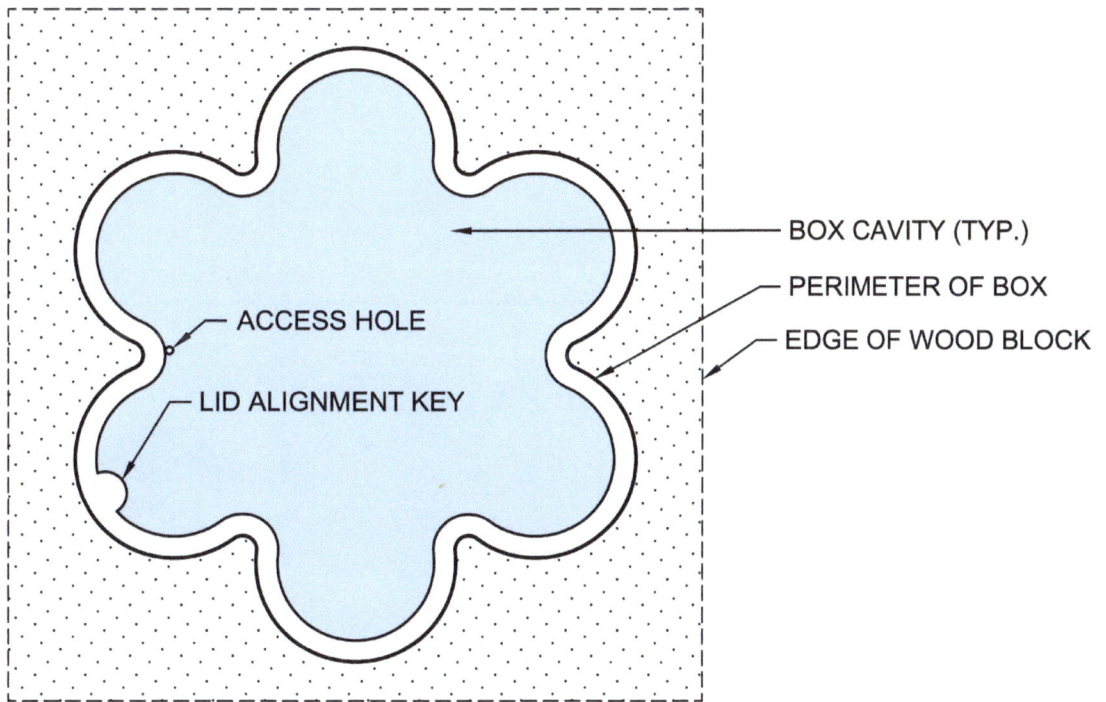

BOX CAVITY (TYP.)

PERIMETER OF BOX

EDGE OF WOOD BLOCK

ACCESS HOLE

LID ALIGNMENT KEY

RADIAL MITOSIS
PATTERN B (BOX CAVITY)

PARALLEL UNIVERSE BOX

WOOD USED:
Box Body - Poplar
Inlays - Soft Maple
Box Top & Bottom - Babinga

5½"

6¼"

BOX TOP

INLAYS (TYP.)

PERIMETER OF BOX

EDGE OF WOOD BLOCK

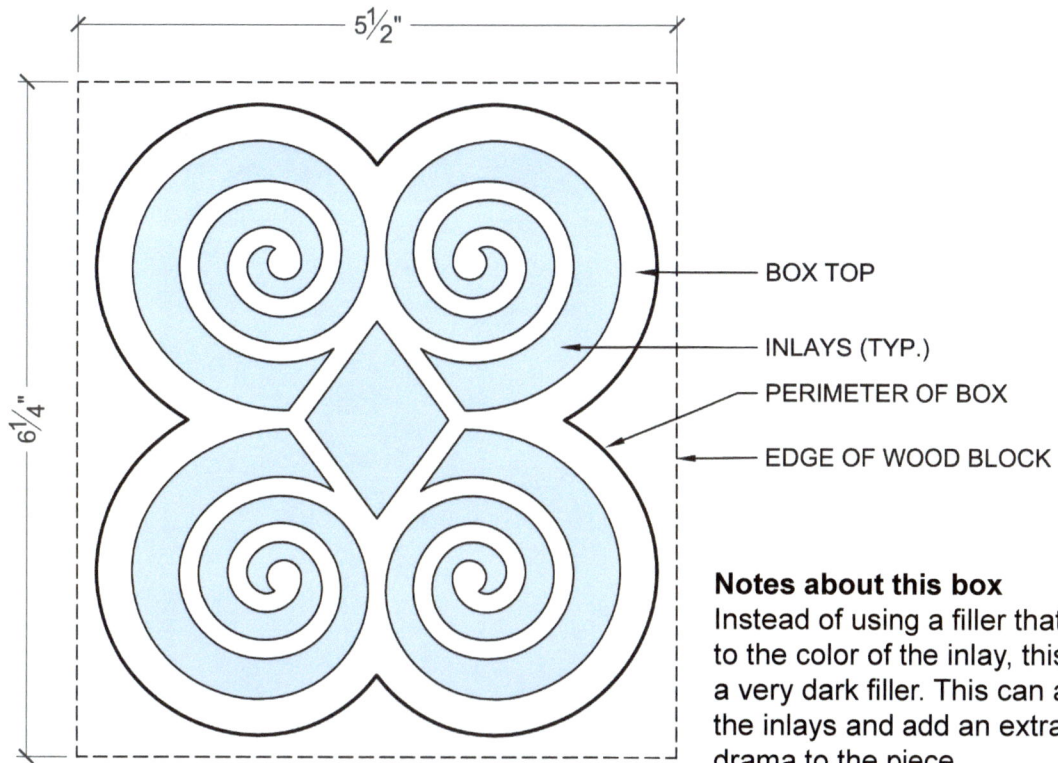

Notes about this box
Instead of using a filler that is similar to the color of the inlay, this box has a very dark filler. This can accentuate the inlays and add an extra layer of drama to the piece.

PARALLEL UNIVERSES BOX
PATTERN A (INLAY)

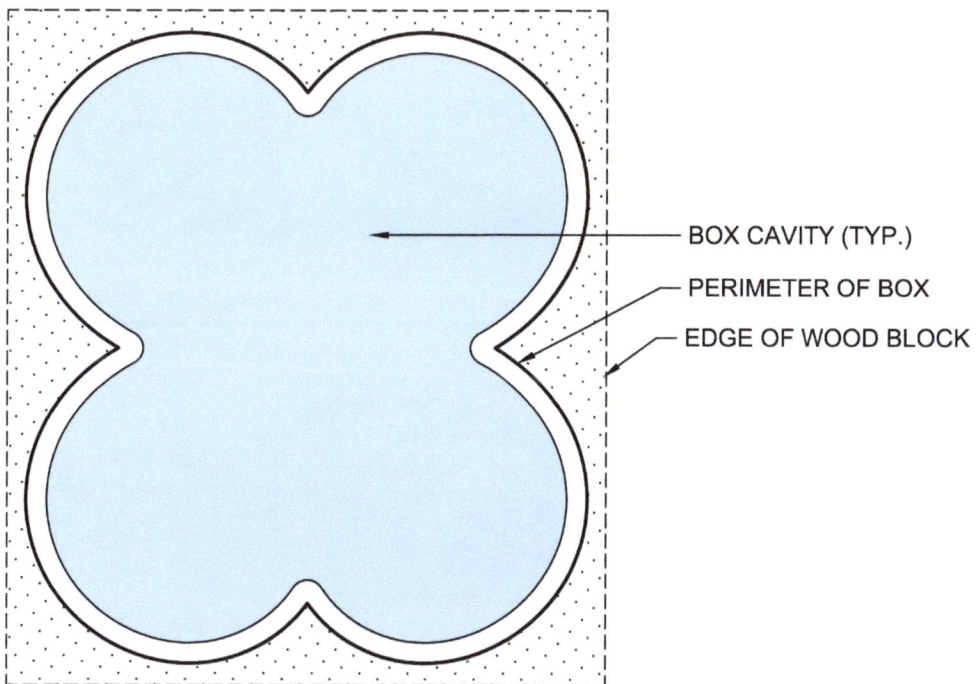

BOX CAVITY (TYP.)

PERIMETER OF BOX

EDGE OF WOOD BLOCK

PARALLEL UNIVERSES BOX
PATTERN B (BOX CAVITY)

VITALITY CONTAINED BOX

WOOD USED:
Box Body - Ash
Inlays - Bird's Eye Maple
Box Top & Bottom - Leopard Wood

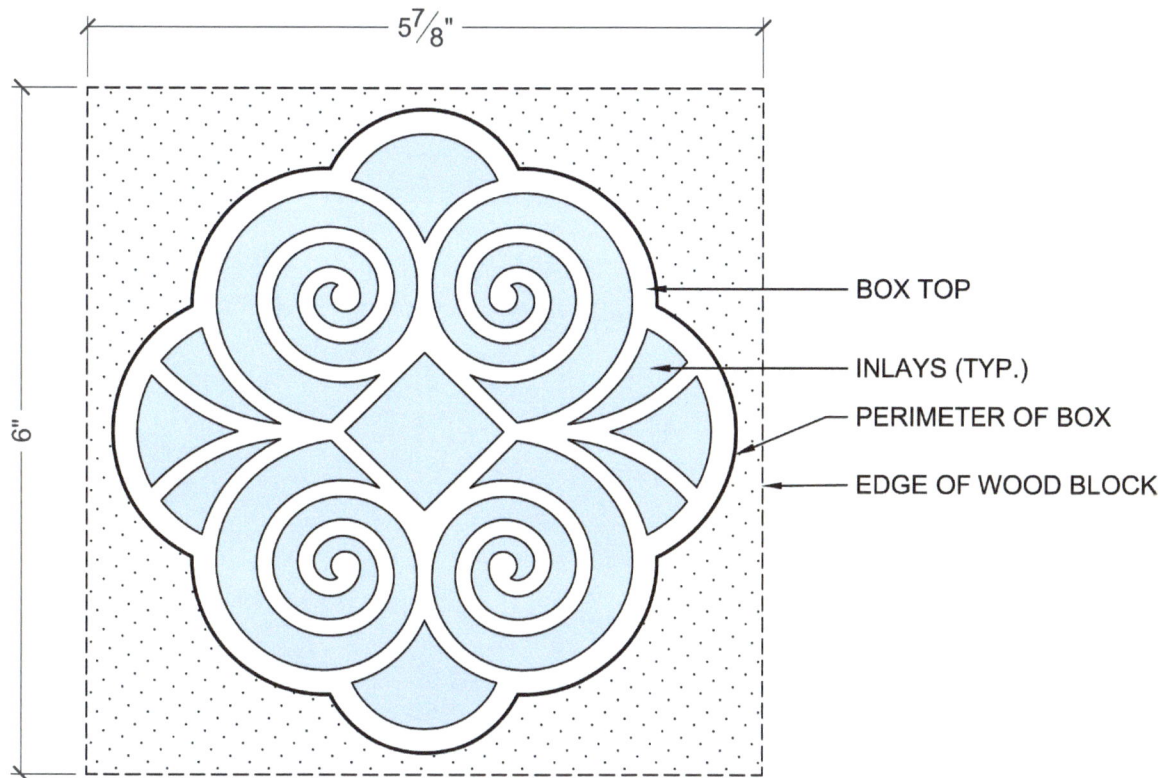

5 7/8"

6"

BOX TOP

INLAYS (TYP.)

PERIMETER OF BOX

EDGE OF WOOD BLOCK

VITALITY CONTAINED
PATTERN A (INLAY)

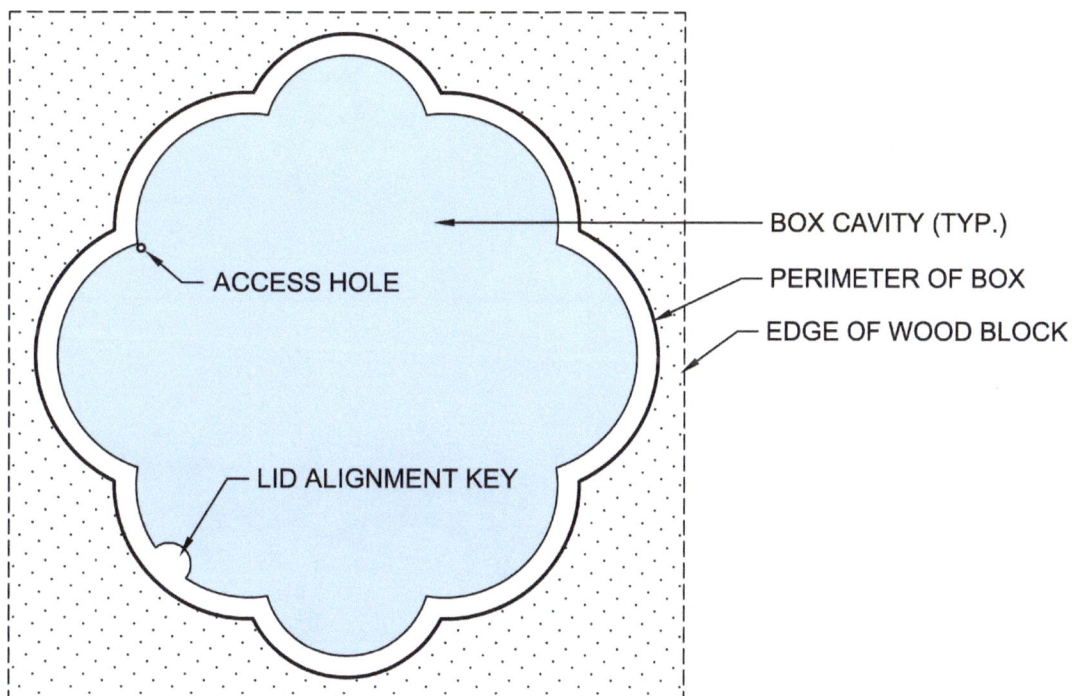

ACCESS HOLE

LID ALIGNMENT KEY

BOX CAVITY (TYP.)

PERIMETER OF BOX

EDGE OF WOOD BLOCK

VITALITY CONTAINED
PATTERN B (BOX CAVITY)

VITALITY UNLEASHED BOX

WOOD USED:
Box Body - Ash
Inlay 1 - Red Heart
Inlay 2 - Purple Heart
Inlay 3 - Black Wood
Inlay 4 - Holly
Box Top & Bottom - Oak

6"

8¼"

BOX TOP

INLAYS (TYP.)

PERIMETER OF BOX

EDGE OF WOOD BLOCK

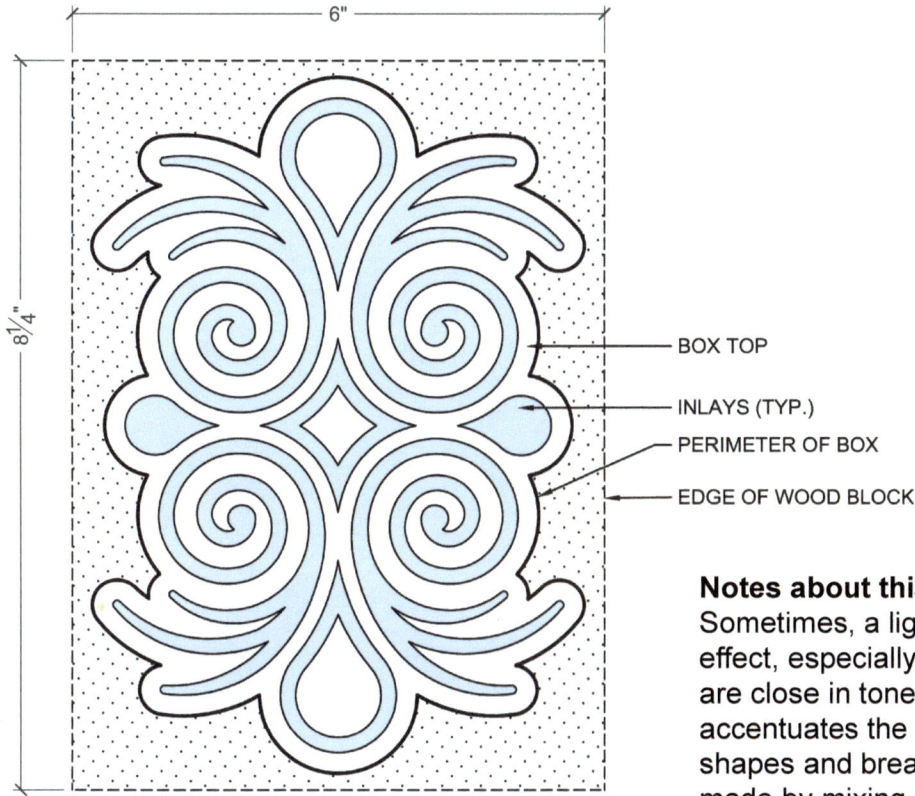

VITALITY UNLEASHED
PATTERN A (INLAY)

Notes about this box

Sometimes, a lighter colored putty can add nice effect, especially if the inlays and the box top are close in tone. For this box, a lighter filler accentuates the inlays, acting as an outline to the shapes and breaking up the colors. Filler can be made by mixing sawdust with wood glue, which is what was done here.

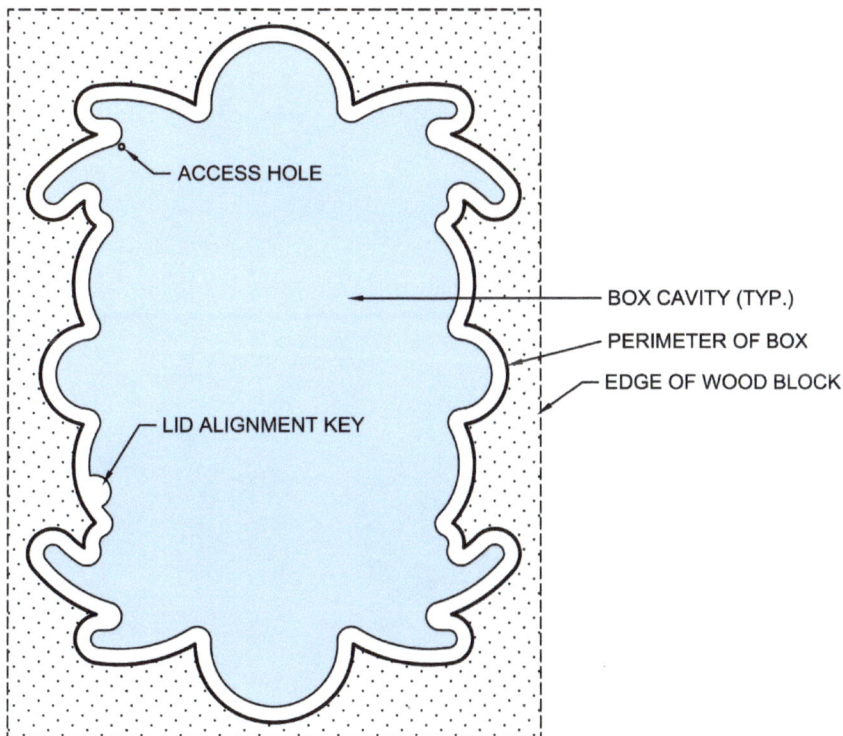

ACCESS HOLE

BOX CAVITY (TYP.)

PERIMETER OF BOX

EDGE OF WOOD BLOCK

LID ALIGNMENT KEY

VITALITY UNLEASHED
PATTERN B (BOX CAVITY)

INTERPLAY BOX

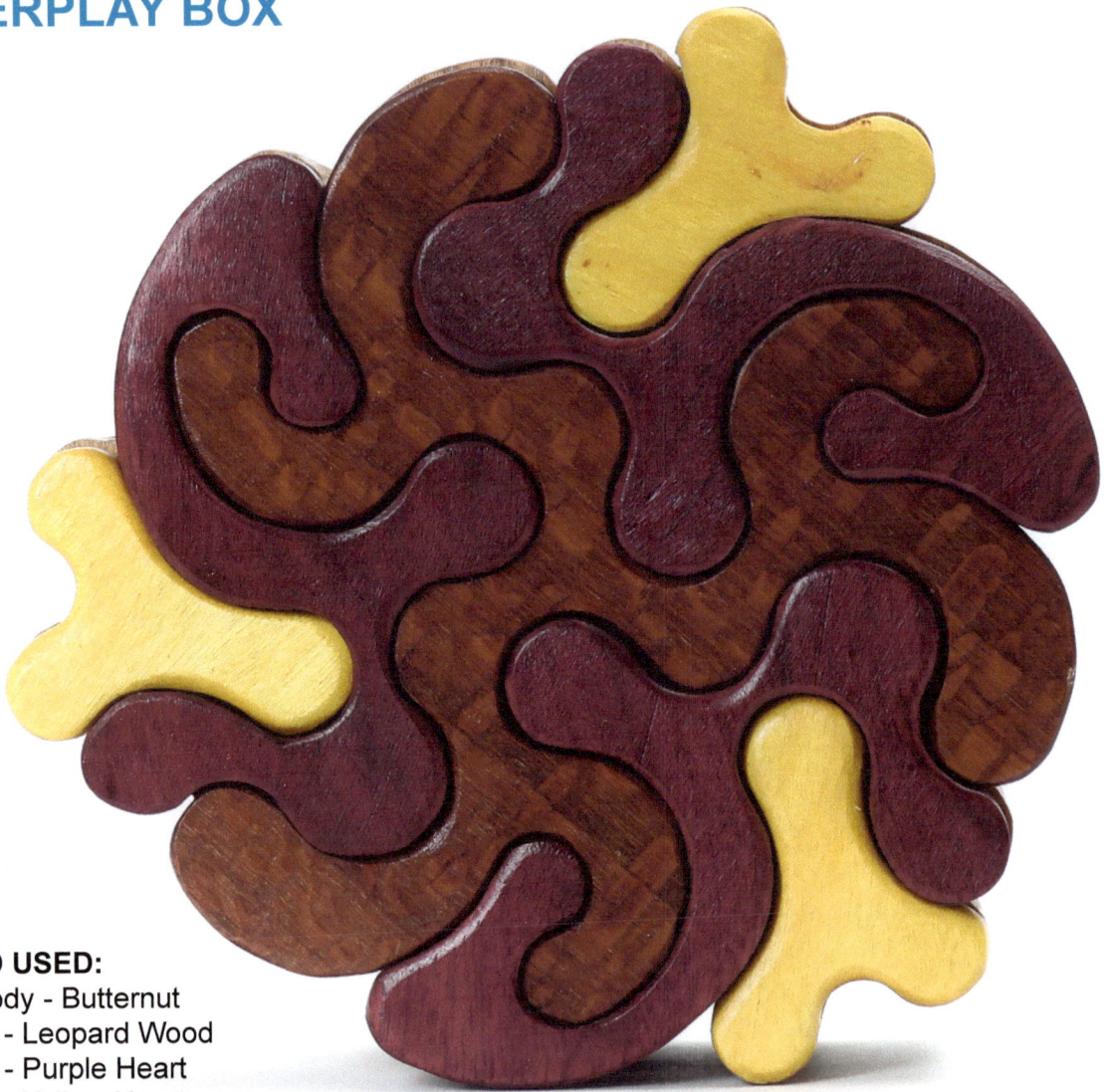

WOOD USED:
Box Body - Butternut
Inlay 1 - Leopard Wood
Inlay 2 - Purple Heart
Inlay 3 - Yellow Heart
Box Bottom - Laminate (various species)

5⅛"

5⅝"

BOX TOP

INLAYS (TYP.)

PERIMETER OF BOX

EDGE OF WOOD BLOCK

Notes about this box
As with some of the other
boxes, the inlay for the purple
heart was thicker than the other
inlays, making it pop up from
the other inlays.

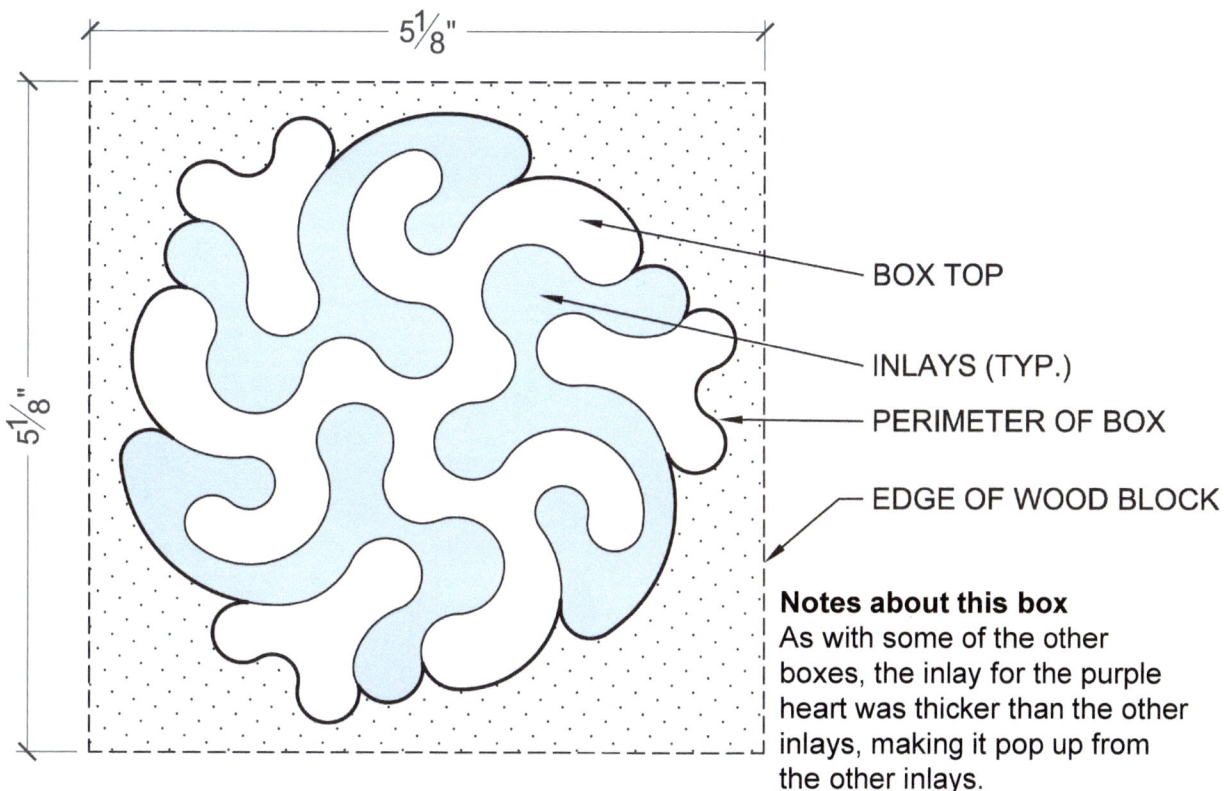

INTERPLAY
PATTERN A (INLAY)

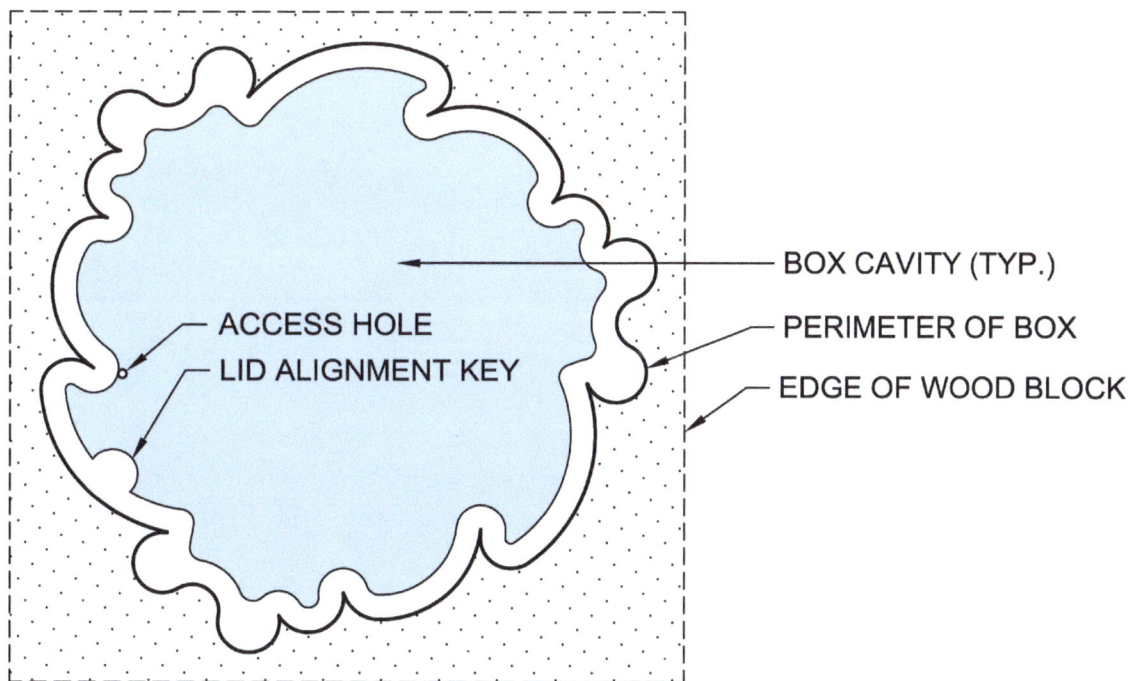

BOX CAVITY (TYP.)

ACCESS HOLE
LID ALIGNMENT KEY

PERIMETER OF BOX

EDGE OF WOOD BLOCK

INTERPLAY
PATTERN B (BOX CAVITY)

DAISY CHAIN BOX

WOOD USED:
Box Body - Soft Maple
Inlay 1 - Purple Heart
Inlay 2 - Yellow Heart
Inlay 3 - Red Heart
Box Top & Bottom - Curly Cherry

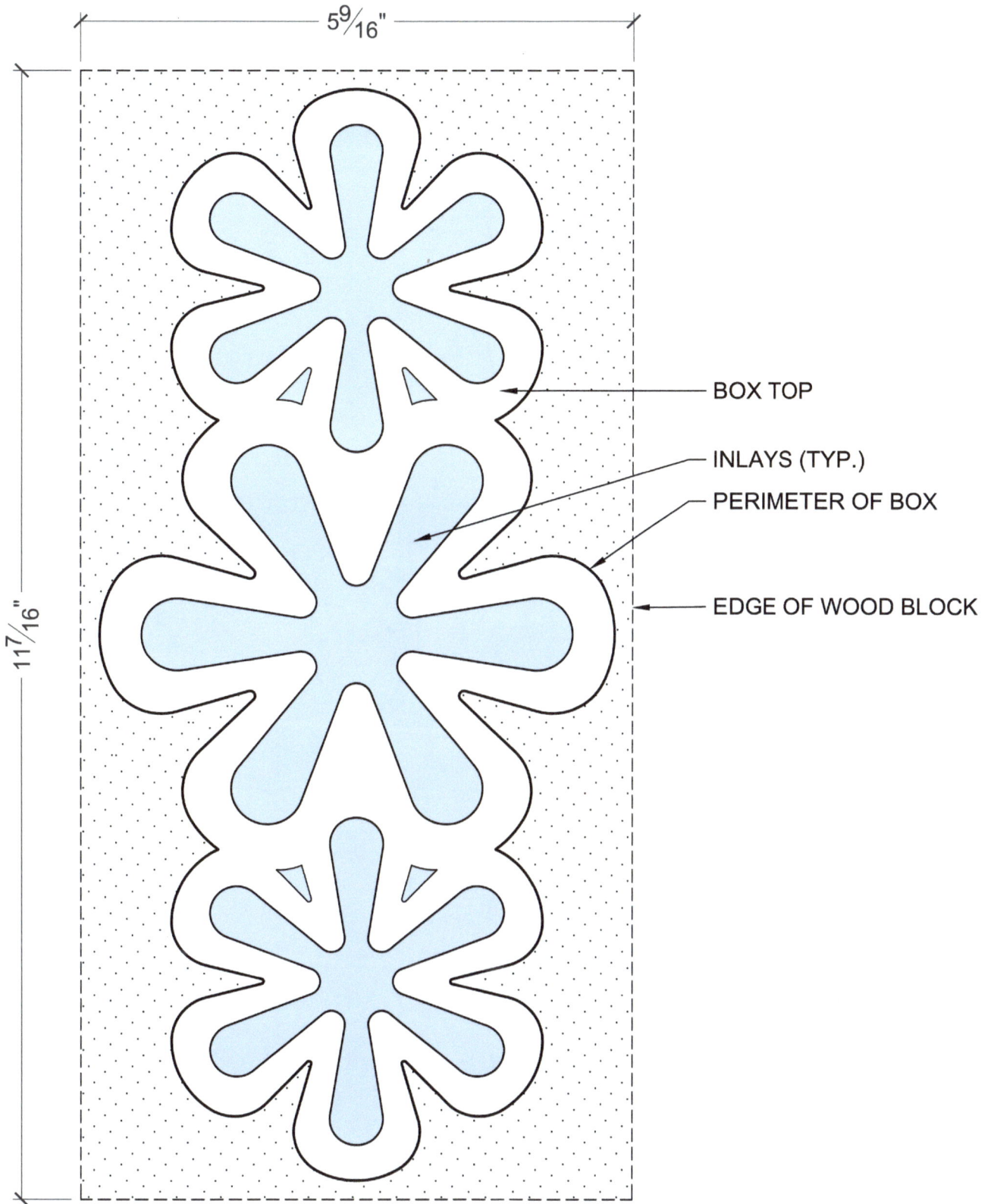

SCROLL SAW INLAY BOXES MADE EASY

5⁹⁄₁₆"

11⁷⁄₁₆"

BOX TOP

INLAYS (TYP.)

PERIMETER OF BOX

EDGE OF WOOD BLOCK

DAISY CHAIN

PATTERN A (INLAY)

Scroll Saw Inlay Boxes Made Easy   49

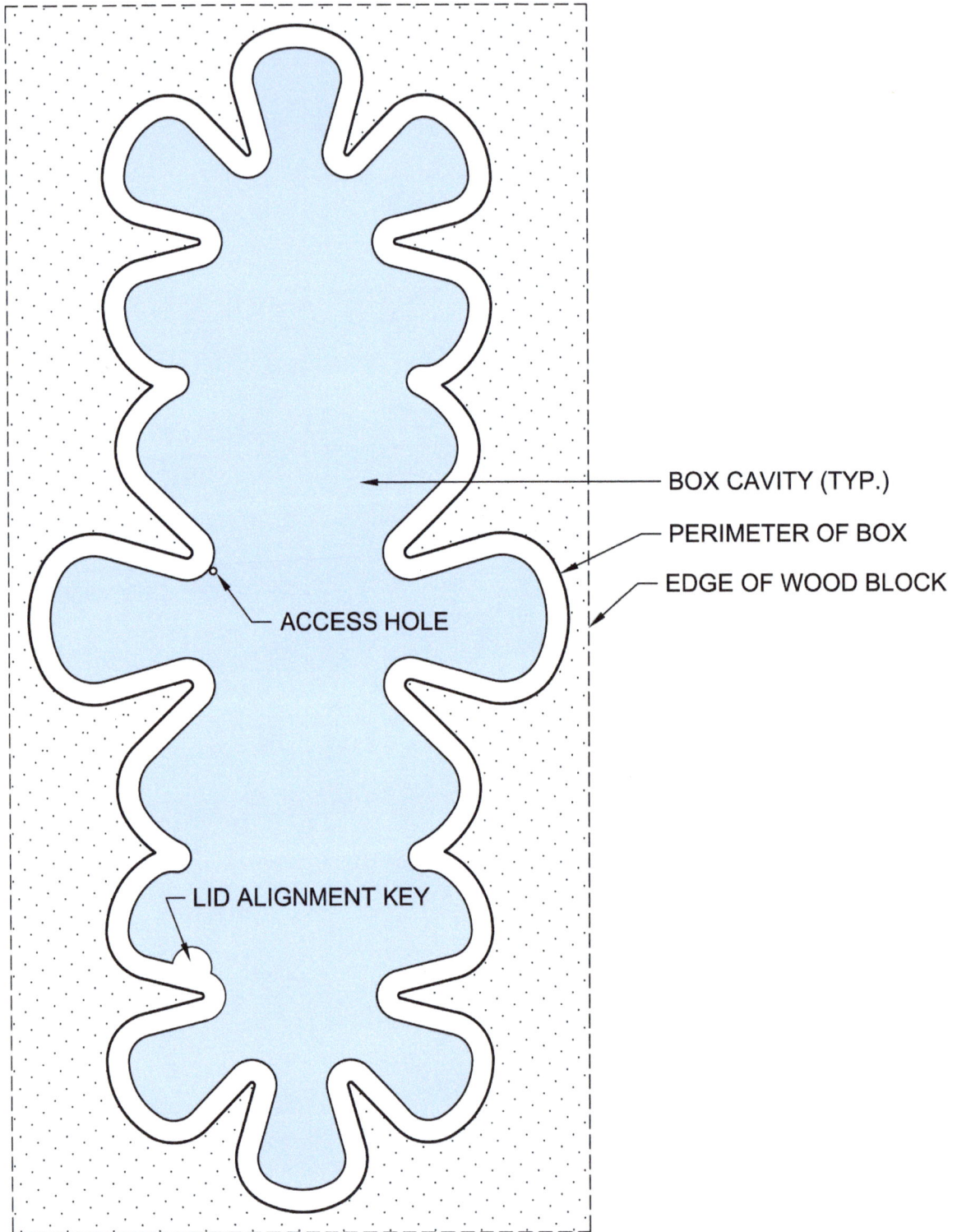

BOX CAVITY (TYP.)

PERIMETER OF BOX

EDGE OF WOOD BLOCK

ACCESS HOLE

LID ALIGNMENT KEY

DAISY CHAIN
PATTERN B (BOX CAVITY)

GET YOUR WORK SHOWN ON OUR WEBSITE

Readers. I hope that you have enjoyed the patterns in this book. I hope also that you have created beautiful boxes and had a great time building them.

If you have, I would love to see them. The boxes in this book were made using a variety of different wood combinations. These combinations can dramatically change how the boxes look. So I would love to see what your boxes look like with your chosen wood combinations.

To show off your wood working skills, I have set up a special section on my wood patterns website just to showcase your work. To get your work shown, e-mail a picture of your box to:

info@modernwoodpatterns.com:

In the e-mail, include your name (as you want it displayed or an alias), the city and state you live in, and what species of wood you have used.

You can see your wood boxes displayed as well as those of other readers. In this way, we can all share our projects and learn from each other.

To all my readers, happy wood working, and be kind to each other.

WWW.MODERNWOODPATTERNS.COM

www.ingramcontent.com/pod-product-compliance
Lightning Source LLC
Chambersburg PA
CBHW042019080426

42735CB00002B/100